BRISTOL MOTOR SPEEDWAY

40 YEARS OF THUNDER

ACKNOWLEDGMENTS

t's been said that race tracks are like people: Each is different and has its own personality. As far as motorsports in the United States is concerned, the race course found in east Tennessee is about as close to the definition of the word "unique" as an auto racing venue can get. There is certainly no other like it allied with NASCAR-sanctioned competition. This is basically why UMI Publications, Inc. is proud to bring you the official "autobiography" of Bristol Motor Speedway.

The track started out over 40 years ago as the dream of two ambitious, young businessmen. They believed that NASCAR auto racing had a definite future in the world of sports and was much more than just a minor "Southern" pastime. From the day the first shovelful of earth was turned through today, enough has happened at Bristol Motor Speedway to fill a book several times larger than the one you're holding.

Yet, with a lot of help, we think we've produced a volume that tells the Bristol story in an informative and captivating way. Much of the credit goes to author Benny Phillips, who drew upon almost four decades of covering NASCAR racing to craft a tale that includes all the principal players.

No book of this type is complete without "artwork." Therefore, we thank everyone who contributed photography that documents the track from Day One right through the 2001 Food City 500 NASCAR Winston Cup race in April. Special thanks go to the Daytona Racing Archives and its curator, Buz McKim; noted free-lance photographers David Allio and David Chobat; CIA Stock Photography's Don Grassman and Ernie Masche and their talented staff, and Fern Greenway of Bristol Motor Speedway, who was instrumental in allowing us to access the track's photo files.

While some people believe that history should stay locked away, others are more than happy to "reopen the books" and make the past come alive once again. In this regard, we can't thank Larry Carrier, Carl Moore, Gary Baker and Warner W. Hodgdon enough for their cooperation.

And without the encouragement and backing of those who make up the heart of the speedway itself, this book would never have happened. Our deepest gratitude goes out to BMS Chairman Bruton Smith and the entire staff at Bristol Motor Speedway and Dragway. Without them, we could never have brought you one of the best stories in American motorsports. A special note of thanks, also, to our good friends at NASCAR including Bill France, Jim France, Brian France, Lesa Kennedy, Paul Brooks, George Pyne, Jennifer White, John Griffin, and Paul Schaefer.

UMI Publications Staff

Ivan Mothershead, President and Publisher; *Charlie Keiger*, Vice President and Associate Publisher; *Rick Peters,* Vice President; *Lewis Patton,* Controller; *Mark Cantey,* National Advertising Manager; *Paul Kaperonis,* Advertising Account Executive; *Ward Woodbury*, Managing Editor; *Merry Schoonmaker,* Senior Associate Editor/Production Manager; *Gary McCredie,* Associate Editor; *Brett Shippy,* Art Director; *Paul Bond,* Senior Designer; *Chris Devera*, Manager of Information Systems; *Mary Flowe,* Administrative Staff; *Joanie Tarbert,* Administrative Staff; *Amy Tosco*, Administrative Staff; *Renee Wedvick*, Administrative Staff

Preproduction work provided by ISCOA (International Scanning Corporation of America). Printed in Kingsport, Tennessee through Quebecor-World.

ISBN 0-943860-20-2

TABLE OF CONTENTS

INTRODUCTION

(Opposite page) From the air, Bristol Motor Speedway, today, could easily be mistaken for a football stadium. Thousands of seats completely ring the high-banked oval called "Thunder Valley." On NASCAR-sanctioned race weekends, not one is empty.

The relationship between Bristol Motor Speedway and what's now the Winston Cup Series dates back to the track's very first event in 1961. It's been a beneficial and enjoyable partnership for all concerned.

We love to dream. We all have had them, those childhood fantasies where, while in the sixth grade, we saved the little girl with bangs from the bully, who sat in the back row next to the door to the hall. So, in a way we still want to do the things we ached to do when we were kids.

Race drivers dream of winning at least half of their circuit's races and 10 straight NASCAR Winston Cup Series championships. Race fans imagine themselves being race drivers, but, unfortunately, that bit of whimsy fades as waistlines expand and reflexes are dulled.

What never disappears, however, and what every race fan dreams of having – or keeping – are race tickets to Bristol Motor Speedway. Each year in eastern Tennessee, NASCAR's knights and their gaudy steel steeds arrive with the clockwork regularity of property taxes and full moons. Both NASCAR Winston Cup Series races –

one in the spring and the other in August – are sold out well in advance. Having precious tickets and suggesting a Bristol trip to anyone who enjoys racing is like inviting a preacher to a screening of what awaits us in the hereafter.

You know how it goes. By late fall you say you've sworn off stock car racing. Then about the middle of February, when a precious few warm afternoons lure you out of the house, and away from the television and – perhaps what is happening in Daytona Beach, Fla. – you begin figuring just how many weekends are left until the first Bristol race.

Throughout the chill of winter, you've probably spent time in your easy chair with coffee and note pads, making lists of upcoming spring projects and materials needed to see them through. But then, as Orion tilts among the spheres off south, you entertain again the notion of the pilgrimage that all true race fans have to make – the trip to Bristol.

You can remember when you didn't have tickets, and when, a few weeks before the race a certain sense of futility crept in, and you began talking about trading your wife's SUV or husband's garden tiller or lawn tractor for four tickets, or, failing that, cutting a deal to swap out Superbowl or Masters tickets with someone you couldn't stand.

Soon the race advances upon us with a quickening that resembles the blur of calendar pages used in old-time movies to show the passing of time. The days grow longer, and the cloak of darkness falls over the last band of ultraviolet sky as it slips down the western ridge. Traffic out front of the speedway twinkles past, and the big trucks begin arriving, loaded with race cars for a full weekend of action.

The next morning the cars snake onto the steeply banked concrete oval for their first taste of the action to come, while down in the pits you can hear the engines revving in the wind as if preparing for liftoff. Fans pour in like corn kernels in a grain bin. This processional continues until every seat is taken. Practice ... time trials ... chatter over the public address system ... the pre-race parade ... then silence just prior to the invocation to ask for the Almighty's protection followed by the Star-Spangled Banner ... the race begins

To close your eyes beneath a flung-back arm and observe with great clarity this towering speedway from above, as a Canada goose passing on set wings might see it; and to hear the engines fussing beneath a delicate summer breeze is something to behold.

Bristol Motor Speedway is the envy of every promoter in racing. Other tracks are publicized wildly and with slogans about their toughness and their speed. Bristol, meanwhile, sits calmly in a picturesque valley and for every Winston Cup event fills every single seat it has, now 147,000, soon to be 165,000. Tickets are sometimes passed on in wills and are issues in divorce settlements. You can't just walk up to the window and buy tickets to a Bristol NASCAR Winston Cup Series race. In 1998, 52,000 tickets in the new Kulwicki Tower sold out in less than three hours.

The first Bristol race was in 1961. Carl Moore and Larry Carrier were responsible for building the track. About to go broke, they sold it to Lanny Hester and Gary Baker of Nashville, Tenn. Baker put up the lights for night racing in 1978. Then Hester and Baker sold the track to Warner Hodgdon, who later filed bankruptcy. This put the track back in the hands of Carrier, who was a trustee at the bank that held the note and was appointed to oversee its operation. Later Carrier bought the track from the bank, kept it several years, and then, in 1996, sold it to O. Bruton Smith. Immediately, Smith went to work with additions and improvements that turned the facility into one of the most modern tracks in automobile racing.

The plan of this book is simple: Take you on a trip that begins with Bristol Motor Speedway's birth up to the present. We've endeavored to make it interesting and easy reading from the first green flag to the final checkered, with just enough "human interest" to complement the story. We hope that when you put the book down, you will know more about your favorite track.

We want you to understand that Bristol Motor Speedway was truly a "build-it-and-they-will-come" sort of thing. To many it must have seemed every bit as bizarre as hacking out a baseball diamond for ghosts in the middle of an Iowa cornfield. The god of pork-barrel projects smiled, however, and in 1961 the track opened with 18,000 seats. Suddenly the locals, who opposed the track,

had to figure out just how one goes about flirting with tourists. It was a fresh, capricious time when towns behaved like an old bachelor who suddenly decides to court the widow down the lane.

East Tennessee communities didn't get into spitting matches over how much better their mountains were than those of Utah or even Europe. They managed. They adjusted. They accepted the track, and the track accepted them. Now it is one big, happy family. Speedway vice president and general manager Jeff Byrd says there are 2,000 community volunteers at the track for every race, and the area chamber of commerce claims the speedway dumps $400 million into the local economy annually.

Fans pour into Bristol twice a year, especially in summer for the night race. They leave with a ton of fresh memories – something to cut and paste into daydreams, something to squeeze like a rubber ball until the next race at Bristol. ∎

(Opposite page, top) Carl Moore (left) and Larry Carrier took an idea and created what turned out to be one of American motorsports' most enduring icons - Bristol Motor Speedway. Their partnership lasted for 17 years.

(Opposite page, middle) Lanny Hester (left) and Gary Baker, here with Darrell and Stevie Waltrip, had a strong impact on Bristol in just a relatively short time. They made improvements to the physical plant, and Baker was responsible for introducing night racing to the track.

(Opposite page, bottom) Bruton Smith, here with seven-time Winston Cup champion, Dale Earnhardt, applied ideas he'd developed in 45 years in the racing industry to BMS when he bought it in 1996. The slogan on the T-shirt is for real!

(Left) What's the secret of Bristol's success as a sporting venue? Ask five people and you'll get as many answers to the question. One answer, though, has to be the racing itself. It's fast, close – and never dull!

BIRTH OF A SPEEDWAY

(Opposite page) One of the first things Carl Moore (left) and Larry Carrier (center) did was hire Hal Hamrick as the track's general manager and public relations representative. Hamrick had a background in radio and television and worked at the speedway until 1965. Today, Hamrick publishes a NASCAR-oriented racing trade paper.

Carrier, Moore and R.G. Pope wanted to build their track in Piney Flats, Tenn., but after encountering opposition from local clergy they settled on this site – a dairy farm – closer to downtown Bristol.

When, during the American Civil War, soldiers in blue marched south, most did double time through Bristol, Tenn. Scouts reported there was little reason to stop, because families in the area were without livestock. Natives of the land smiled as the bluecoats rode out of sight. Tucked away in mountain coves, overlooked by Union scouts, were more fine horses than Gen. Ulysses S. Grant ever knew existed. Prime beef cattle and fat dairy cows grazed in lush meadows and drank from rippling trout streams. Hidden from the world by mountain peaks and evergreen forests, the animals were safe from the hated enemy.

The track born as Bristol International Speedway, once known as Bristol International Raceway, and today called Bristol Motor Speedway, sits in one of these valleys where locals drove their livestock to hide them from Yankee soldiers. After the "War Between the States"

ended in 1865, the property became a dairy farm for most of the next century. Cows might still be grazing and milk trucks hauling their product to town had it not been for two young entrepreneurs.

Larry Carrier grew up in Bristol and Carl Moore in nearby Kingsport. Carrier, the son of Mr. and Mrs. Robert Hugh Carrier, built and ran three bowling alleys at one time, and he constructed more than 600 houses in the northeast Tennessee town. Carrier and Carl Moore became friends and invested in a couple of small businesses, but were looking to do more and bigger things. They put their heads together to build the speedway. Their stewardship lasted almost two decades.

"We were in business together for 27 years," Carrier said. "We built the track in 1960 and opened the place in 1961. We had a third party in R.G. Pope, but he sold his share to us after the first year."

"We were in business together for 27 years," Carrier said. "We built the track in 1960 and opened the place in 1961. We had a third party in R.G. Pope, but he sold his share to us after the first year."

Once the three partners secured a loan for $600,000, construction began. Tons of earth had to be moved, an oval was carved out and soon the once quiet country-side reverberated with the sound of racing twice a year.

"It was a Saturday afternoon, and I was in Knoxville for a University of Tennessee football game," Moore remembered. "Larry called me from Charlotte. 'I am down here for an automobile race,' he said. 'They have a new speedway, and you can't believe the number of people here – and they're paying $20 a ticket to see the race. You

ought to come down here tomorrow. I think this might be something we want to consider for an investment.' So I went to Charlotte the next day."

That was 1960, and the more the two young men talked, the more they convinced themselves that a race track would be a good investment.

(Above) Miss Firebird "flew in" for the first race in July 1961.

(Top left) Carrier (left) and Moore (right) knew how to attract celebrities. They introduced driver Junior Johnson (next to Moore) to world heavyweight boxing champ Rocky Marciano.

(Far left) The tow hitch had to be removed from Doug Yates' 1961 Plymouth before the first race. Yates started 26th and finished 19th in the 42-car field.

(Left) Rex White, the 1960 Grand National champion, ran seven races at Bristol. He finished second to Joe Weatherly in the '61 Southeastern 500.

Volunteer 500
· · · · ·
July 30, 1961

*I*t was a historic day, that hot afternoon in July of 1961. The new Bristol International Speedway was open for business. "Fearless Freddie" Lorenzen would start from pole position in a Holman-Moody Ford. Riding shotgun on the front row was the legendary Junior Johnson in a Pontiac.

Johnson took the lead on the first lap and led through lap 124. Lorenzen's Ford experienced differential (rear end) problems. He never led and finally finished 33rd. Johnson led again, lap 180 through 225, but ended up with a 22nd-place finish.

Jack Smith, in the No. 46 1961Pontiac, gets credit for the victory, although Johnny Allen took over in relief of Smith and drove 209 of the laps. Smith got out of his car because he said the floorboard was getting hot and that he burned his right foot. Allen, who dropped out of the race on lap 107 after his Chevrolet caught fire, took over for Smith and averaged 68.373 mph for the 500 laps.

Fireball Roberts finished second in a Pontiac, more than two laps behind. Ned Jarrett was third in a Chevrolet, Richard Petty fourth in a Plymouth, and Buddy Baker fifth in a Chrysler.

Forty-two cars started the historic race and 19 finished.

Southeastern 500
· · · · ·
October 22, 1961

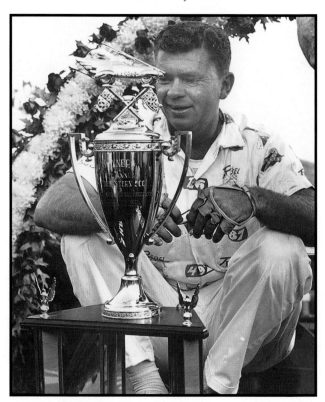

*I*t was the peak of the colorful autumn season in east Tennessee when Bristol International Speedway staged its second race. Junior Johnson crossed over the mountain ridges from Ronda, N.C., and stole the show that afternoon but did not win the race. Instead, "Little Joe" Weatherly drove a Bud Moore-prepared Pontiac to victory, winning by several car lengths over Rex White in a Chevy. It was the Virginian's 12th NASCAR Grand National career victory and third in the last six races. Nelson Stacy was third in a Ford, Jim Paschal fourth in a Pontiac, and Emanuel Zervakis rounded out the top five in a Chevy.

Bobby Johns won the pole in a Pontiac, but Johnson, also in a Pontiac, took the lead on lap 31 and led through lap 212. He led again from lap 283 through lap 394 and was five laps out in front of everybody when differential problems sidelined him for the day. Weatherly led from lap 419 to the finish, averaging 72.452 mph, and winning $3,680.

Ned Jarrett finished sixth, nine laps down. He held an 894-point lead over White and clinched the title for 1961.

(Left) Bobby Johns admires his hardware. Johns, from Miami, Fla., won the 1962 Volunteer 500 in a car prepared by his dad, Shorty (left).

(Bottom left) Jim Paschal dodges an errant tire during the 1961 Volunteer 500. He finished eighth in this Pontiac owned by J.H. "Julie" Petty, Richard Petty's uncle.

(Below) DeWayne "Tiny" Lund gives Rex White a "lift." White raced from 1956-64 and retired; Lund raced from 1955 until his death in 1975.

Carl Moore was well acquainted with many of NASCAR Winston Cup racing's early drivers, including Edward Glenn "Fireball" Roberts, considered by many today to be the circuit's first superstar. True to form, the Florida ace didn't wait long to win at Bristol. He captured the 1963 Southeastern 500, and had he not died from racing injuries received at Charlotte the following year, most likely he would have been even more successful on the Tennessee track.

"It was strictly a financial adventure for us," Moore said. "We were not fans. We were looking at it only from a business standpoint."

Volunteer 500
·····
April 29, 1962

*M*iami, Fla.'s "Little" Bobby Johns didn't win often, but when he did, he won big. On this spring afternoon, he led 430 of the 500 laps, winning by six laps, to post his second victory in the major-league division of stock car racing. Johns was driving a No. 72 Pontiac prepared by his father, Shorty. Fireball Roberts, in a Pontiac, finished second, Jack Smith was third in another Pontiac, Ned Jarrett fourth in a Chevrolet, and Tom Cox fifth in a Plymouth. The top 10 was rounded out by Herman "The Turtle" Beam, Ford; David Pearson, Pontiac; Wendell Scott, Chevrolet; Bill Morton, Ford; and Curtis "Crawfish" Crider in a Mercury.

Richard Petty, who led on two occasions when Johns made his pit stops, fell out while running second on lap 368 because of a blown engine. He ended up finishing 16th. Others in the 36-car field who weren't around to receive the checkered flag included Fred Lorenzen, Junior Johnson, Buck Baker, Ralph Earnhardt and Richard's younger brother, Maurice, who crashed on the 298th lap.

Johns started sixth and averaged 73.397 mph. Roberts, who won the pole at 81.374 mph, and R. Petty were the only other race leaders. A crowd of 17,000 fans was on hand to see Johns win and collect the first-place prize of $4,405.

Southeastern 500
·····
July 29, 1962

*V*eteran Jim Paschal (above) had just joined the Petty stable and was on his first mission, in a blue No. 42 Plymouth, during the 1962 season. He wheeled around Fred Lorenzen's No. 20 Holman-Moody Ford with 26 laps to go and pulled away to a half-lap advantage on his way to victory in just the fourth race ever run at Bristol Speedway. Lorenzen's car lost a wheel in a shower of sparks on the final lap, but the ace from Illinois still collected second-place money of $2,370.

Richard Petty was third in a Plymouth, Johnny Allen fourth in a Pontiac, and Nelson Stacy fifth in a Ford. Completing spots six through 10 were Joe Weatherly, Rex White, Bunkie Blackburn, Ned Jarrett and Jimmy Pardue. Junior Johnson led two times for 246 laps before his No. 6 Cotton Owens Pontiac blew and tire and crashed on the 284th lap.

En route to the 1962 Grand National championship, Weatherly left the track 1,786 points in front of Petty. Weatherly had qualified 13th fastest but because of ingrained superstition refused to line up in that position for the start. The race promoter fixed things by giving "Little Joe" starting spot No. "12a."

Paschal's average speed came to 75.276 mph for the 500 laps. Fireball Roberts won the pole position with a speed of 80.321 mph.

"We could not get a bank in the area to sit down and talk with us,"

Moore recalled. "Nobody wanted any part of a race track. We wanted to

build one, but we needed $600,000."

Carrier (right) didn't "miss" a lick when he brought Weatherly and his car owner, Bud Moore, into victory circle after Weatherly won in October 1961. "Miss Southeastern 500" (right), "Miss Firebird," "Miss Bristol International Speedway" and an unidentified "Miss" (left) all enhanced the occasion.

"It was strictly a financial adventure for us," Moore said. "We were not fans. We were looking at it only from a business standpoint."

They talked R.G. Pope, the owner of a construction company, into joining them. So off they went in search of property.

Bristol International Speedway almost became "Piney Flats International Speedway." The group was ready to come in and start moving dirt when a couple of local preachers expressed their indignant opposition. They feared the type of people the race track might draw to Piney Flats and vicinity. Carrier, Moore and Pope did not want hand-to-hand combat with two church congregations,

so they waved the white flag and pulled up stakes. Larry's father, was a real estate broker. He found another tract of land, a dairy farm, five miles down the road, closer to Bristol. The three investors took an option on the 100 acres. Then they figured the total cost for the project, including land, would be $600,000. Now they faced another dilemma. They didn't have any money.

"We could not get a bank in the area to sit down and talk with us," Moore recalled. "Nobody wanted any part of a race track. We wanted to build one, but we needed $600,000."

Those area bankers who would not loan them money now have suites at the speedway.

(Above) Jimmy Pardue ran the first eight races at Bristol and finished sixth twice. He died at Charlotte in 1964 during a tire test.

(Far left) Bobby Johns was one of NASCAR racing's most well liked drivers in the 1950s and '60s. He started 141 races and won two, including one at Bristol.

(Left) "Gentleman" Jim Paschal raced out of High Point, N.C., and won 25 Winston Cup races from 1953-67. Included was the 1962 Southeastern 500.

(Below left) When Junior Johnson raced this Chevrolet at Bristol in 1963 for car owner Ray Fox Sr., pit stops were more "relaxed" than they are today. Johnson became the most successful car owner to ever compete at the track.

(Below) Marvin "Pancho" Panch won 21 poles and 17 Winston Cup races from 1951-66, but none at Bristol. Running for the Wood Brothers, he started and finished fourth in the 1963 and '65 Volunteer 500s.

Southeastern 500
• • • •
March 31, 1963

*T*he powers that be changed things around at Bristol and decided to run the Southeastern 500 as the first race of the year rather than the second.

That suited the Florida ace, Fireball Roberts, just fine. He switched from a Pontiac to a No. 22 Holman-Moody Ford the week before the race and drove by his new teammate, Freddie Lorenzen, to win his first event at the half-mile track. Roberts, who started third behind Lorenzen and DeWayne "Tiny" Lund, averaged 76.910 mph.

There was obviously no great love lost between the two Holman-Moody drivers. Roberts used every drop of fuel in his car to win, while Lorenzen was forced to make a quick pit stop for just enough gas to finish. He said he couldn't figure how his car went 110 miles on a full tank during one portion of the race and just 85 on another.

During one portion of the event, Lorenzen hit Roberts' car hard enough to knock the fuel filler cap off. Roberts had to pit and then run 164 laps to get back into the lead.

Junior Johnson finished third in a Pontiac, Richard Petty fourth in a Plymouth, and LeeRoy Yarbrough fifth in a Mercury. Jimmy Pardue, Darel Dieringer, Billy Wade, Bud Harless and Joe Weatherly completed the top 10.

Thirty-five drivers started the Southeastern 500, but only 13 were around at the checkered flag. And as in the preceding race here, Joe Weatherly again qualified 13th fastest. This time, though, he had to start in spot No. 13 and not in position "12a."

Volunteer 500
• • • •
July 28, 1963

*F*red Lorenzen, a factor so many times, finally drove his Holman-Moody Ford to victory on this July afternoon. Lorenzen, who started on the pole, beat Plymouth-driving Richard Petty by three seconds. Jim Paschal, Petty's teammate in another Plymouth, was third. Marvin Panch was fourth in a Ford, and David Pearson rounded out the top five in a Dodge.

Fireball Roberts wrenched his back in the most spectacular wreck in the three-year history of the half-mile track. His Holman-Moody Ford hit the wall on the 312th lap and turned end over end four times. Roberts got out of the car, walked to the infield and fell on his knees (above). He was taken to a nearby hospital where he spent the next several hours.

Junior Johnson led all of the event's first 161 laps except one but bad luck struck him again. For the 12th time in 20 races, he was forced behind the wall – this time with a blown engine. Other race casualties included Billy Wade (clutch); Jack Smith (engine failure); Buck Baker (ignition); Nelson Stacy (crash) and Possum Jones (brakes). Still, 21 of the 36 starting drivers were around at the checkered flag.

Lorenzen took 3 hours, 20 minutes and 25 seconds to complete the race at an average speed of 74.844 mph and won $4,540. A crowd estimated at 23,000 filled the grandstands.

Southeastern 500
· · · · ·
March 22, 1964

F red Lorenzen became the first two-time winner at Bristol. He led 494 of the 500 laps to win in a smoking No. 28 Holman-Moody Ford that crossed the finish line at 60 mph. Lorenzen beat teammate Fireball Roberts by half a lap. Paul Goldsmith, in a Plymouth, was third, Buck Baker in another Plymouth was fourth, and Marvin "Pancho" Panch – the pole winner (80.640 mph) – in a Ford was fifth.

En route to his first win of the 1964 Grand National season, the Elmhurst, Ill., driver passed Panch on the seventh lap and motored away never to be passed again. Then with just 24 laps left, smoke began trailing from under Lorenzen's Ford. Later he said he "didn't know if he was going to make it or not," noting that it "was something in the engine."

Ned Jarrett, Jim Paschal, Richard Petty, Rex White and Billy Wade rounded out the top 10.

It was the second time in a week that Lorenzen had survived engine failure. While cruising at 11,000 feet, an engine in his Beech Bonanza private aircraft let go in a spectacular manner. At first he was startled, but then a cooler head prevailed. Lorenzen backed off on the power and completed the trip to Chicago. He said it was a "close call."

Volunteer 500
· · · · ·
July 26, 1964

R ichard Petty had a three-lap lead over Fred Lorenzen when his engine failed on lap 496. Petty puttered around for three laps and his car quit on pit road on lap 499. Petty got out of his car and watched Lorenzen take the checkered flag.

Lorenzen led only the last lap of the race in his Ford. Petty was second, in a Plymouth, Jim Paschal third in a Plymouth, LeeRoy Yarbrough fourth in a Dodge and Larry Thomas fifth in a Ford, eight laps down. Jimmy Pardue, Marvin Panch, Roy Mayne, Buddy Arrington and J.T. Putney completed the top 10 finishers.

Petty started from the pole. After passing Junior Johnson on lap 351, Petty worked his way into a three-lap lead. Then four laps from the finish, his 1964 Plymouth began trailing smoke. Petty coaxed it along but fell one lap short. His second-place finish was worth $2,730.

Lorenzen was still recovering from the effects of an accident he had in the Firecracker 400 in Daytona Beach, Fla., about three weeks before. Ned Jarrett, who dropped out early, relieved Lorenzen on laps 276-443. After a refreshing rest, Lorenzen got back in and finished the race in 3 hours, 12 minutes and 12 seconds at an average speed of 78.044 mph.

Carrier and Moore had to go out of town for their $600,000 loan. "We finally went to New Jersey to talk with a man who ran concession stands for some football stadiums," Moore said. "We didn't ask how else the man made a living. "I remember he wore big rings and smoked long cigars. I had never smoked a cigar in my life, but I smoked two or three that day. He loaned us the entire $600,000. The interest rate (offered by financial institutions) was six percent at the time,

and he charged us 12 percent. We also signed over concession rights to him for the first 15 years of operation."

Now they had the money but no blueprints. They scribbled on brown paper bags and envelopes. "We had no real plans," Moore said. "R.G. was a contractor, and he and Larry cut through two mountains to make room for the track. We went from one day to the next, and things went pretty well. When we ran out of money, we quit."

(Top) Here, Fred Lorenzen was leading the 1963 Southeastern 500, but he ended up finishing second to teammate Fireball Roberts, who drove the No. 22 Holman-Moody Ford.

(Above) Lorenzen definitely knew how to handle the track's high groove during the July 1963 Volunteer 500. He led most of the laps and won his third race of the year. Jack Smith (47) dropped out with a blown engine.

(Above right) Bobby Isaac (left) drove eight races for Junior Johnson in 1966, Johnson's final season as both a race driver and team owner.

(Right) Isaac and Paul Goldsmith (25) were teammates when they drove at Bristol in 1964 for Ray Nichels.

Southeastern 500
· · · · ·
May 2, 1965

*J*unior Johnson won his first race at Bristol (and as it would turn out, his only one as a driver), and he took a chance by running on tubeless tires, a first in NASCAR racing. Johnson, driving a No. 26 Ford, also survived a fender-crunching battle with Holman-Moody Ford driver Dick Hutcherson about 50 laps from the finish. Hutcherson finished second. The top five were all Ford drivers, with Ned Jarrett third, Marvin Panch fourth and Wendell Scott fifth.

Almost everyone left the track thinking the win was Johnson's fourth of the season. One exception was native Iowan Hutcherson, who said Johnson was a lap down at the finish and that he actually finished second, with Hutcherson in first.

At 265 laps, Johnson had to pit because of a blown tire and lost one and one-half laps. Next, he needed relief driving help from Fred Lorenzen for 147 laps. Hutcherson maintained that Johnson had lost two laps while turning the car over to Lorenzen and had made just one of them back up. But after watching a scoring recheck, Ralph Moody, one of "Hutch's" car owners, agreed with the official result.

That didn't placate Hutcherson, however, who said "Robert E. Lee's grandson was scoring the race."

Johnson, who said running the tubeless tires was an experiment that paid off, averaged 74.937 mph in the 3-hour, 20-minute and 10-second race and won $4,500. Rounding out the top 10 were Junior Spencer (Ford); J.T. Putney (Chevrolet); Jabe Thomas (Ford); E.J. Trivette (Chevrolet) and Gene Black (Ford.)

Volunteer 500
· · · · ·
July 25, 1965

*T*he drivers did their best while the weather was at its worst. Ned Jarrett drove to victory in the No. 11 Bondy Long-owned Ford despite eight caution flags, mostly for rain. It was the eighth win of the season for 32-year-old North Carolinian, who was battling for his second series title.

Dick Hutcherson and Sam McQuagg finished second and third, respectively. Both drove Fords. Jim Paschal was fourth and Buck Baker fifth. Both were in Chevrolets. Fred Lorenzen started from the pole.

The race was not an easy contest for the winner and many others. A series of crashes and rain delays slowed things for 167 of 500 laps. Included were four red-flag periods. Tempers flared and Hutcherson ended up losing his second consecutive Bristol race by just one position.

The race also marked the end of Chrysler Corp.'s factory team boycott, but the two main players didn't fare too well. David Pearson (Cotton Owens Dodge) crashed out after just eight laps, and Richard Petty (Petty Engineering Plymouth) dropped out with rear-end problems and finished 17th after starting second.

Junior Spencer, Wendell Scott, Donald Tucker, Bob Derrington and J.T. Putney rounded out the top 10 in a race that took over four hours to complete.

The three finished work in time to open their new NASCAR-sanctioned speedway in July 1961. The place had 18,000 seats and a little press box on top of the main grandstand. According to Moore, nearly every seat was filled for that first race.

"I guess we had about 17,000 fans," he said. "We charged $3, $4 and $5, and the purse was $90,000. All the drivers stayed at the Holiday Inn in Bristol, and there were several of them who never did anything but party the whole time," Moore said.

They named the two races Volunteer 500 and Southeastern 500. Fred Lorenzen won the pole for the first Volunteer 500 with a speed of 79.225 miles per hour. Forty-two cars started the event, and only 19 finished. Jack Smith, with relief help from Johnny Allen, won the $3,025 first-place purse.

When built, the track had 22-degree banking and measured a half-mile around. Moore and Carrier weren't satisfied and paid visits to a couple of tracks looking for ideas. They were thinking of something much steeper than the relatively flat half-miler in Martinsville, Va. – and they wanted their speedplant to be the fastest half-mile track in the world. Workers reshaped the track after the 1969 fall race. What they came up with was a "bowl" with 36-degree banking in the turns, the steepest in all of NASCAR. The new design also "stretched" the track to 0.533-mile, which meant 500-lap races increased from 250 to 266.5 miles.

(Top right) Native Midwesterner Darel Dieringer was always a fan favorite during his heyday in the 1960s. He won the pole for the 1967 Southeastern 500, in Junior Johnson's Ford, and finished third.

(Bottom right) Jim Paschal (41) feels the heat from Junior Johnson during the '64 Volunteer 500. Billy Wade relieved Paschal to finish third, while Johnson's Banjo Matthews Ford suffered a blown engine.

(Below) Darel Dieringer (16) qualified 10th fastest for the 1965 Volunteer 500. Junior Johnson put his white Ford in the third place on the starting grid, one spot behind Richard Petty's Plymouth. None of them, though, would take the checkered flag.

The three finished work in time to open their new NASCAR-sanctioned speedway in July 1961. The place had 18,000 seats and a little press box on top of the main grandstand. According to Moore, nearly every seat was filled for that first race.

(Above) Wendell Scott dropped out of the 1964 Volunteer 500 after completing just 41 laps. He kept up with the race, though, by listening to it on the radio!

(Above left) Fred Lorenzen (28) and Richard Petty put on a classic Ford–Plymouth duel in the 1965 Volunteer 500. Both, however, failed to finish the race.

(Left) Two of the top racing celebrities of the 1960s were driver Curtis Turner (left) and Ralph Moody, 50 percent owner of the famed Holman-Moody Ford "racing factory" in Charlotte.

Southeastern 500
· · · · ·
March 20, 1966

*T*his event featured seven caution flags for 92 laps, with only seven cars finishing out of a starting field of 32.

Dick Hutcherson (middle), after finishing second twice in a row at Bristol, won the race in the No. 29 Holman-Moody Ford. Paul Lewis finished second in a Plymouth, James Hylton was third in a Dodge, Elmo Langley took fourth in a Ford, and Sam McQuagg ended up fifth in a Dodge.

David Pearson (right) started from the pole in a No. 6 Dodge owned by Cotton Owens and led 330 of the first 382 laps. He slowed on lap 383 with a broken timing chain, was credited with a 15th-place finish and Hutcherson led the rest of the way. It was the first win of the year for the 34-year-old Iowan and the 10th of his career.

"When David went out, I knew all I had to do was finish the 500 laps to win it," Hutcherson said. "We had blown an engine on Thursday and another one on Friday. I just backed off and coasted home."

Gene Black finished sixth in a Ford, 24 laps down, while Bill Seifert was seventh, 43 laps behind the winner. Credited with finishing eighth through 10th were Wendell Scott, Henley Gray and G.C. Spencer. Bobby Isaac (left) crashed out of his third straight race but was unharmed.

It was not a good day for the leading drivers of the circuit. Ned Jarrett, Marvin Panch, Paul Goldsmith, Bobby Allison and Fred Lorenzen all dropped out because of one problem or another.

Volunteer 500
· · · · ·
July 24, 1966

*R*ichard Petty had taken the lead on lap 160, by lap 376 was ahead by three circuits, and then neck cramps got to him. Petty called on Jim Paschal, who had dropped out of the race with engine failure, for relief at the wheel. Petty and Paschal lost their advantage while in the pits swapping places in the driver's seat, and Paul Goldsmith drove by and on to victory. He was in a Plymouth as was Petty, who was credited with finishing second. David Pearson was third in a Dodge, Paul Lewis fourth in a Plymouth, and Bobby Allison fifth in a Chevrolet.

Curtis Turner started from the pole after qualifying at 84.309 mph. His race ended, however, on the 210th lap because of engine failure.

Southeastern 500
· · · · ·
March 19, 1967

*D*avid Pearson, driving Cotton Owens 1967 Dodge, won the race – his first of the year – but had to come from behind with nine miles left.

It seemed Dick Hutcherson was on his way to victory when his engine blew on lap 482. He led Cale Yarborough by one lap and Pearson by two. Then Yarborough ran over some debris and blew a tire. He decided to try to finish the race running on the inner-liner.

Yarborough led through lap 494, but his gamble failed when Pearson made the pass for the win. Yarborough finished second in the No. 21 Wood Brothers Ford. Darel Dieringer, who won the pole at 87.124 mph, finished third in Junior Johnson's '67 Ford, followed by Neil Castles in a Plymouth and Hutcherson.

"There wouldn't have been any question about it if my front tire hadn't gone flat," said Yarborough, who was looking for his second career victory. "David could never have passed me."

Completing the top 10 were Elmo Langley, in a Ford; Donnie Allison, in a Chevrolet; Bill Seifert, Ford; Wendell Scott, Ford; and Max Ledbetter, Chevrolet.

It took Pearson 3 hours, 17 minutes and 32 seconds to complete the event at an average speed of 75.937 mph and collect $5,290. Thirty-six drivers started the race and 11 finished.

Volunteer 500
· · · · ·
July 23, 1967

*R*ichard Petty started from the pole in his No. 43 Petty Enterprises Plymouth and won the race. Sounds easy, doesn't it?

Well, it wasn't. Petty had a tire go down and he lost two laps. Then the crew left the cap off the gas tank and he lost another lap. But as was so common in those days, Petty staged a comeback which returned him to the lead on lap 256. He took the lead for good on lap 439 and won by three-quarters of a lap. It was the Randlemen, N.C., driver's third straight win in, for him, a very good season.

Dick Hutcherson finished second in a Ford, followed by Darel Dieringer in another Ford. Jim Paschal was fourth in a Plymouth and James Hylton rounded out the top five in a Dodge. Rounding out the top 10 were Neil Castles, Elmo Langley, Friday Hassler, "Big John" Sears and Buck Baker.

It took Petty 3 hours, 10 minutes and 35 seconds to win at an average speed of 78.705 mph.

(Right) Richard Petty motors on by in the 1966 Southeastern 500 as Bobby Isaac exits the No.26 Junior Johnson Ford after he crashed on lap 204.

(Far right) When a photographer at Bristol caught David Pearson (left) and Fred Lorenzen relaxing before a 1967 race, both were at the top of their game.

(Right) Pro football's interest in NASCAR racing is nothing new. Famed Baltimore quarterback Johnny Unitas was a special guest at Bristol for the Southeastern 500 in 1967.

(Below) Fred Lorenzen (pole) and Richard Petty paced the field for the 1965 Volunteer 500, a race that was won by Ned Jarrett.

(Right) Larry Carrier (left) and mechanic Herb Nab seem to enjoy Curtis Turner's "do" before the July race in 1966. In his only start at Bristol, Turner started on the pole but failed to finish.

"**W**e talked with Pat Purcell, executive vice president of NASCAR," Moore said. "Pat said if we had the guts to build a track, he would give us the dates for two races."

Southeastern 500
• • • • •
March 17, 1968

*S*outh Carolina's David Pearson (who would end the year with his second Grand National championship) had left Dodge and joined the Holman-Moody Ford team.

It took 10 months for him to get to victory circle, but he did it on this Sunday afternoon, taking the lead 31 laps from the finish. Richard Petty finished second, in a Plymouth, just a few car lengths back. LeeRoy Yarbrough was third in the Junior Johnson-owned Ford, followed by Darel Dieringer in a Plymouth. Bobby Isaac rounded out the top five in a Dodge.

The race was something of a classic duel that saw Pearson and Petty swap the lead four times. Petty led 108 of the 500 laps but couldn't match the performance of his "Petty Blue" Plymouth. The car was stout, but Petty was worn out at the finish.

"The car had what it took to win, but the driver didn't," Petty admitted. "I was so tired, I wasn't driving as sharp as you need to be here."

Pearson qualified second fastest while Petty started on the pole. The caution waved 11 times for 81 laps.

Volunteer 500
• • • • •
July 21, 1968

*T*he mercury climbed to 95 degrees on this Sunday afternoon with track temperatures reaching 140. David Pearson appeared to ignore the weather; he started sixth and took his time while the heat took its toll on man and machine.

After the track got hot and slick, Pearson's car seemed to handle better, and he drove the No 17 Holman-Moody Ford to his second straight victory here. Cale Yarborough in the Wood Brothers Mercury finished second. Swede Savage, in the Bondy Long Ford, was third. Bobby Isaac was fourth, in a Dodge, and Friday Hassler was fifth in a Chevrolet.

LeeRoy Yarbrough (above) started from the pole, but his No. 98 Junior Johnson Ford succumbed to engine failure on the 121st lap and finished 32nd in a 36-car field.

Pearson completed the race in 3 hours, 16 minutes and 34 seconds at an average speed of 76.310 mph.

The one thing the promoters didn't have a problem with back then that today can create sticky situations is obtaining Winston Cup Series race dates. "We talked with Pat Purcell, executive vice president of NASCAR," Moore said. "Pat said if we had the guts to build a track, he would give us the dates for two races."

After the first race, Carrier and Moore bought the stock owned by R.G. Pope, who, it seemed, might have had a good idea in "getting out." The two remaining partners found it difficult to get fans back to their track. "There was no point fund to amount to anything, no ESPN, and people didn't buy advance tickets," Moore recalled. "I guess Larry put up signs on every power pole in the country. At least, it seemed like he did. Also, back then you had to deal with every driver about coming to your race. They wanted appearance money ... anywhere from $500 to $5,000."

(Above) The main entrance to Bristol International Speedway on Highway 11 East certainly looked a lot different in the 1960s than it does today. Back then, fans could drive in about when they wanted to buy tickets, look around or just pass the time of day. Today, there are several "main" entrances.

(Right) NASCAR President Bill France Sr. (left) stayed in touch with his track promoters, including Moore. France turned control of the sanctioning body over to his son, Bill Jr., in 1972 and passed away 20 years later.

(Below right) Richard Petty (43) swoops on by Darel Dieringer (26) and James Hylton late in the 1967 Volunteer 500. Petty won the race, Dieringer, in Junior Johnson's Ford, finished third, while Hylton was fourth.

(Far right) Richard Petty stopped long enough here to let his father, Lee, offer a bit of advice. Lee, of course, was the founder of NASCAR's most famous racing dynasty.

Southeastern 500
· · · · ·
March 23, 1969

*W*ith less than 30 miles to go, mechanical failures sidelined both Bobby Isaac and David Pearson. This opened the door for Bobby Allison (right) to drive to victory in the Mario Rossi-prepared Dodge in front of 28,000 screaming fans.

Allison was four laps in front of runner-up LeeRoy Yarbrough's Ford at the end of the race. David Pearson was third, in a Ford, Cale Yarborough fourth, in a Mercury, and the winner's "little brother," Donnie Allison (left), took fifth in a Banjo Matthews-owned Ford.

Isaac started from the pole and led 299 laps before his engine failed. Pearson was leading with 15 laps to go and had engine problems. While Pearson treated his misfortune as just that, Isaac was so upset over his foul luck that he ran across the track, jumped over the guardrail and disappeared into a parking area.

Completing the top 10 were Dave Marcis (Dodge), Richard Petty (Ford), Elmo Langley (Ford), Friday Hassler (Chevrolet) and Neil "Soapy" Castles (Plymouth).

Allison's "lucky" 13th career victory was worth $5,025. He finished the race in 3 hours, 4 minutes and 9 seconds at an average speed of 81.455 mph.

Volunteer 500
· · · · ·
July 20, 1969

*W*hen NASCAR's top division arrived ready to run the ninth annual Volunteer 500, its competitors were faced with an entirely "new" Bristol International Speedway. Track management had put a different face on the track by increasing the banking in the turns from 22 to 36 degrees, the steepest of any track on the circuit. This increased the speed in qualifying about 15 miles an hour over the spring race.

Cale Yarborough, in the Wood Brothers Mercury, won the pole at a speed of 103.432 mph, and flu-stricken David Pearson, with relief-driving help from Richard Petty (above), won the race in a Ford. Petty, who went out early with engine problems, took over for Pearson and led the final 142 laps. Only 10 cars finished the race, and 10th-place Roy Tyner was 97 laps down.

Bobby Isaac was second, three laps behind, in a Dodge. Donnie Allison was third in a Ford, James Hylton fourth in a Dodge, and Cecil Gordon fifth in a Ford.

"There was no point fund to amount to anything, no ESPN, and people didn't buy advance tickets," Moore recalled. "I guess Larry put up signs on every power pole in the country. At least, it seemed like he did."

According to Moore, there was a complete lack of support. "One year we had all the drivers coming, and David Pearson (a young, crowd-pleasing hotshoe) had not sent in his entry blank. I picked up the local paper one morning and there was a big headline, 'Pearson Will Not Race At Bristol.' The paper did not say anything about who would race at Bristol.

During his first "term" as a race promoter, Larry Carrier (left) was energetic and innovative. He was also on good terms with NASCAR boss Bill France Sr., who appreciated Carrier's hard work. While a lot of short tracks were removed from the Winston Cup Series schedule at the start of the so-called "modern era" in 1972, Bristol wasn't one of them.

"We discovered, too, that people would wait until Sunday morning to buy tickets. If it was cloudy, the newspaper would be calling for rain on the Sunday of our race. They just killed us at times."

Today, Carolyn Carrier handles public relations for Winston Cup driver and team owner Brett Bodine. She's been involved in motorsports for years but still remembers what it was like being Larry Carrier's daughter. "Daddy drove a car with Bristol Speedway logos all over it," she said. "Mother would take us to school in the car, and we would beg her to let us out about a block from school. If she drove up in front of the school to let us out, all the other kids would make fun of us that day."

(Top) The pace car driver and his passenger watch David Pearson (17) go by with Richard Petty in hot pursuit. Pearson won the 1968 Southeastern 500 by finishing three seconds in front of Petty.

(Above) The wrecker removes G.C. Spencer, who crashed early in the '68 Southeasten 500. Bill Seifert (45) was 12th.

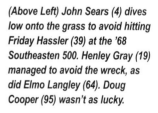

(Above Left) John Sears (4) dives low onto the grass to avoid hitting Friday Hassler (39) at the '68 Southeasten 500. Henley Gray (19) managed to avoid the wreck, as did Elmo Langley (64). Doug Cooper (95) wasn't as lucky.

(Middle Left) Tiny Lund does his best to stay ahead of Stan Meserve (51) and Jerry Grant at the '68 Southeasten 500. Both Lund and Meserve were the victims of engine failure.

(Bottom Left) "Move over, Darel!" LeeRoy Yarbrough (26) puts pressure on Darel Dieringer in the '68 Southeasten 500. It worked, as Yarbrough passed Dieringer to finish the race one spot ahead – third.

Southeastern 500
· · · · ·
April 5, 1970

*T*his one was an Allison brothers show. Donnie Allison (above) took the lead late in the event and drove to his third career victory in a Banjo Mathews-owned Ford. Bobby Allison finished second, three laps behind, in a Don Robertson Plymouth he'd rented for the race. Cale Yarborough was third in a Mercury, even though its engine blew up 44 laps shy of the finishing distance, James Hylton was fourth in a Ford and Dick Brooks fifth in a Plymouth.

Richard Petty, back in a Plymouth after a one-year defection to Ford, lost his lead in Grand National points when he got too close to Yarborough and Ed Negre early on and crashed. J.D. McDuffie and Henley Gray were sixth and seventh, respectively, in a Buick and a Ford, Cecil Gordon finished eighth in a Ford, Coo Coo Marlin was ninth in a Chevrolet and 10th, also in a Chevrolet, was Ken Meisenhelder.

David Pearson won the pole in a Ford but dropped out on the 181st lap with a blown engine.

Volunteer 500
· · · · ·
July 19, 1970

*T*he word "relief" really meant something in the 28th race of the 1970 NASCAR Grand National season.

In another scorcher in "Thunder Valley," Bobby Allison (left) started 10th in his own 1969 Dodge, but it was Dave Marcis (right) who took over in relief for the final 130 laps and finished two laps ahead of LeeRoy Yarbrough's Junior Johnson Ford to win the race.

The heat had also gotten to Yarbrough, so it was Donnie Allison who brought the car home in second place. Bobby Isaac finished third in a Dodge, G.C. Spencer was fourth in a Plymouth, and Pete Hamilton rounded out the top five driving relief for Richard Petty!

After Allison saw his rivals calling for help, he got the message and decided imitation was not flattery – it was smart!

"I saw what LeeRoy and Petty were doing. I decided I was foolish to try it myself," he said. "It was hot and I was getting tired. I saw Marcis in my pit, and I couldn't think of anyone I'd rather have in my car."

The five drivers who finished sixth through 10th all drove their own cars. In order, they were Frank Warren (Plymouth), Bill Champion (Ford), Elmo Langley (Ford), J.D. McDuffie (Mercury) and Cecil Gordon (Ford).

Eight caution flags for 54 laps slowed the race to 84.880 mph. Cale Yarborough, involved in a wreck, started from the pole in a Mercury. The Allison-Marcis combo took 3 hours, 8 minutes and 23 seconds to go from the first green to the checkered.

Southeastern 500
· · · · ·
March 28, 1971

Volunteer 500
· · · · ·
July 11, 1971

You never know what to expect at Bristol Speedway. Richard Petty (above) had a lap-and-a-half lead when a wheel came off his Plymouth with 80 circuits remaining. He lost a lap and then nearly chased down David Pearson for the victory. But as it turned out, Pearson, who made a couple of mistakes of his own, won by four seconds over Petty.

Pearson took off when the green flag dropped, led the first 48 laps and when a car spun around in the first corner, he pitted for what he thought would be a caution flag. The race stayed green, though, and when he got back onto the track, his Holman-Moody Ford was a lap down.

After overcoming that problem, he tangled with another car on the 181st lap, spun out but somehow managed to recover and go after Petty. He succeeded and landed in victory lane for the 60th time.

Petty was in a Plymouth. Dick Brooks finished third, in a Dodge, 11 laps down, Bobby Allison was fourth, also in a Dodge, and Benny Parsons, with relief from G.C. Spencer, rounded out the top five in a Ford. Completing the top 10 were Friday Hassler, Elmo Langley, Jabe Thomas, Henley Gray and Neil Castles.

Pearson, who started on the pole, completed the event in 2 hours, 52 minutes and 23 seconds at an average speed of 91.704 mph in front of 25,000 fans. His share of the purse was $6,120.

The team of Charlie Glotzbach (above) and relief driver Friday Hassler shared victory lane, winning over Bobby Allison by three laps.

The race was memorable in that, one, there were no caution periods and, two, it was the first time Chevrolet had won in three years. The winning car was prepared by Junior Johnson and was owned by Charlotte Motor Speedway General Manager Richard Howard. Glotzbach was credited with the victory. His winning average speed was 101.074 mph, which still remains the track record speed.

After Hassler got into the car, he lost the lead to Allison three times but refused to quit. After taking over for good on lap 357, the No. 3 ran like a rocket on wheels.

The car led 411 of the 500 laps. Glotzbach passed pole-winner Richard Petty on lap 44 and led through lap 255 when he pitted and Hassler took over. Allison was in a Holman-Moody Ford. Petty was third in a Plymouth, Cecil Gordon fourth in a Mercury, and James Hylton fifth in a Ford. Completing the top 10 were: Elmo Langley (Ford); Frank Warren (Ford); Bill Champion (Ford); J.D. McDuffie (Mercury) and Jabe Thomas (Plymouth).

The record run by Glotzbach and Hassler was worth $5,675.

To a kid in that position today, riding in a "pace car" would be something of a status symbol!

"We built the drag strip, and we never turned a profit at either place," Moore noted. "We never made any money in racing. We used the track for a rodeo and had an exhibition football game between the Washington Redskins and Philadelphia Eagles. We didn't make any money on either. We even had a country music festival. It looked like a sure thing. The weather was good. I sat there on a bale of hay for three days and said, 'Where are the rest of the people?'" Part of the problem was that Moore and his partner were "three or four years too early for everything. Both of us kept our daytime jobs and just kept borrowing more and more money."

Moore said that he and Carrier "had notes at every bank in town," and their enterprise had turned into a "cash drain." They ran into financial problems and, after the 1976 season, sold the facility to Gary Baker and Lenny Hester, two businessmen from Nashville. ■

(Above) G.C. Spencer checks his lap times from a practice session for the 1970 Volunteer 500. Spencer was admired by many, including Darrell Waltrip, who called him "my hero."

(Above right) Bobby Allison (12) races to put some distance between himself and Bobby Isaac in front of a throng of fans in the "economy" seats.

(Right) This pit stop by Coo Coo Marlin in the 1975 Volunteer 500 was just a little out of sync, but he brought the Cunningham-Kelley Chevrolet home for a seventh-place finish. Coo Coo's son, Sterling, who worked in the pits that day, would drive in his first Winston Cup race the next year.

Southeastern 500
· · · · ·
April 9, 1972

Bobby Allison beat Indy Car star A.J. Foyt a week before at Atlanta, and he dominated this race, leading 458 of the 500 laps and winning by more than four circuits. He was driving a No. 12 Coca-Cola-sponsored Chevrolet owned by Junior Johnson, making it the second straight Bristol victory for the North Carolina promoter.

Only four drivers led the race, and Coo Coo Marlin passed Bobby Isaac on lap 33 for the day's only lead change under the green flag. Isaac finished second in a Dodge, Richard Petty was third in a Plymouth, LeeRoy Yarbrough was fourth in a Ford and Cecil Gordon fifth in a Mercury.

Allison's dominance elicited complaints over the technical rules from Isaac, Petty and others. A NASCAR spokesman countered that since the sanctioning body was pleased with the level of competition, there would be no changes.

"We win two races, and everybody's saying we have an advantage," noted Allison. "I guess that's to be expected."

The Hueytown, Ala., driver, was, of course, in a great mood. Not only had he roughed up a pair of North Carolina rivals, his wife, Judy was on hand (above) personally to congratulate him in victory lane.

"Local" favorite Coo Coo Marlin completed 473 laps and finished sixth, Elmo Langley was seventh; James Hylton, eighth; G.C. Spencer, ninth; and Jabe Thomas was 10th, 38 laps behind the winner.

Volunteer 500
· · · · ·
July 9, 1972

Bobby Allison had things working his way in the Chevrolet owned by Junior Johnson and prepared by Junior Johnson, who (above) joined his ace in the hole in victory lane. After winning the spring race, he came back to Bristol in the summer and won again, this time by more than three laps. He led 445 of the 500 laps, again after starting from the pole position.

Allison got around Richard Petty's Plymouth on lap 210 and led the rest of the way. At the finish, the Level Cross, N.C., "king" was three laps down.

"It was good to have a cushion, but it's hard to win, lose or draw at this track," Allison noted. "It beats you to death each time."

Dave Marcis was third in his own 1970 Dodge; Benny Parsons fourth in an L.G. DeWitt 1971 Mercury; and J.D. McDuffie fifth in a 1970 Dodge owned by Dr. Donald Tarr.

Allison averaged 107.279 mph in winning the pole, and 92.735 mph in winning the race.

(Top right) Cale Yarborough defined Winston Cup racing in the 1970s. He was a tough, unrelenting but personable driver who won nine poles at Bristol and as many races.

(Middle right) "I don't know, Coo Coo, it don't look like a scorpion." Coo Coo Marlin (left) might be wanting to know where Richard Petty gets his "driving boots!"

(Bottom right) The Bud Moore Ford of Buddy Baker and Richard Petty No. 43 Dodge started 1-2 in the 1975 Southeastern 500. Petty won and Baker finished third.

Anything can happen at Bristol, as this photo sequence from the 1974 Southeastern 500 illustrates. When Dean Dalton (7) plowed into Richard Petty (43) the mishap also swept up L.D. Ottinger (02) and Dave Marcis (2). Bobby Allison (12) and Donnie Allison (88) were able to get by unscathed.

(Top left) Buddy Baker excelled on super-speedways, but he was no slouch on the short tracks like Bristol, either. He lapped the track at 110.951 mph to win the pole for the 1975 Southeastern 500. He finished third in the Bud Moore Engineering Ford behind Benny Parsons and winner Richard Petty.

(Top) Travis Tiller came into the pits during the 1975 Southeastern 500 when the engine in his Dodge overheated. A crewman tried to cool it off by spraying it with water to no avail.

(Above) Richard Petty (43) puts another lap on Dave Marcis during the 1975 Southeastern 500. Petty won and Marcis finished eighth, eight laps off the pace.

Southeastern 500
•••••
March 25, 1973

While 1972 saw Bobby Allison – in the Richard Howard/Junior Johnson Chevrolet – dominate both Bristol races, it looked like Cale Yarborough had picked up where the Alabama driver had left off.

Almost nobody ever dominated a field of race cars like Cale Yarborough did on this Sunday afternoon. He started from the pole and led the entire race to win by more than two laps over Richard Petty. It was the first time since 1967, when Darel Dieringer led all the way at North Wilkesboro, N.C., that anyone had led a NASCAR Winston Cup race flag to flag.

"I've never had an easier ride – never," an elated Yarborough said. "I've been fortunate to have driven some fine race cars through the years. I must say I've never had a smoother ride over this long a race.

"When that happens on a short track, it's something else."

Petty was in a Plymouth; Allison finished third in his own Chevrolet; Dave Marcis was fourth in a Dodge; and Benny Parsons fifth in a Mercury. Rounding out the top 10 were Lennie Pond, Coo Coo Marlin, James Hylton, Vic Parsons and John A. Utsman. Yarborough won the pole with a speed of 107.608 mph and averaged 88.952 mph in the race. His share of the pot was $8,030. There were seven cautions for 56 laps and 32,500 in attendance.

Volunteer 500
•••••
July 8, 1973

It was hot as blazes. Only five drivers went the distance without relief, and "newcomers" took over at the speedway.

Benny Parsons, who was actively chasing after the championship, won only the second race of his career but had to have help from John Utsman, a local Sportsman star, who relieved Parsons for 170 laps. Parsons, however, got back into his No. 72 L.G. DeWitt Chevrolet and completed the final 80 laps or 43 miles.

Newport, Tenn.'s L.D. Ottinger, driving in his second major league race, finished second in a Chevy, but he was more than seven laps behind the winner. Cecil Gordon was third in a Chevy, Lennie Pond fourth in a Chevy, and J.D. McDuffie rounded out the top five in another Chevy.

"It was terribly hot out there today and everybody was calling for relief," Parsons, who was beginning his fourth full year in Grand National racing, said in victory lane. "I was glad a guy as capable as John was standing by.

"He kept the car out front."

Cale Yarborough won the pole at 106.472 mph in the Richard Howard Chevrolet but crashed out on the 344th lap and finished 19th.

(Top) Pole winner Buddy Baker, in the No. 15 Bud Moore Engineering Ford, and Richard Petty, in the No. 43 Petty Enterprises Dodge, paced the field at the start of the 1975 Southeastern 500 on March 16. Twenty-three cars started the race, Petty won it and Baker finished third, seven laps down.

(Above left) There was no sponsor on Moore's No. 15 Ford when Baker drove it in the '75 season's second race, the Volunteer 500 in November, and Baker had to park the car on the 90th lap because of an engine problem.

(Above right) Benny Parsons (72) was credited with a fifth-place finish in theVolunteer 500, although he was relieved by John A. Utsman.

(Right) A photographer caught Cale Yarborough getting into his No. 11 Junior Johnson Chevrolet before the start of the 1975 Volunteer 500. Yarborough started on the pole, led the race three times for 171 laps but was sidelined by a sour engine on the 284th circuit.

(Below) Bobby Isaac drove the No. 3 Ed Gibson Chevrolet sponsored by Richard Howard's furniture store in the '75 Volunteer 500, as did Dick Brooks in the No. 90 Truxmore-sponsored Junie Donlavey Ford.

(Right) Bill Champion, a well known "independent" driver/owner of the era, didn't fare too well in '75 Volunteer 500. The engine in his 1973 Ford blew up on lap 387, and he collected $635 for a 17th-place finish.

Southeastern 500
· · · · ·
March 17, 1974

*T*here was an "energy crisis" gripping the nation and people were waiting in long lines at gasoline service stations. That, along with snow flurries and chilly weather, however, didn't stop a long line of Chevrolets, with Cale Yarborough up front, make this a St. Patrick's Day event that fans would remember.

En route to his second victory of the young season, Yarborough took the lead from Bobby Allison on lap 191 and never looked back.

The first 10 cars across the finish line were Chevys with Yarborough leading the way in the No. 11 Junior Johnson-prepared racer. Bobby Isaac was second, Benny Parsons third, B. Allison fourth and Donnie Allison fifth. Spots sixth through 10 were taken by Cecil Gordon, Joe Mihalic, James Hylton, Alton Jones and Coo Coo Marlin. It was the first time in the history of the 26-year-old NASCAR Winston Cup Series that one make of car had swept the top 10 positions.

A jarring crash on the 109th time around the high-banked track saw point leader Richard Petty eliminated from the race. Petty emerged unscathed, as did L.D. Ottinger, but Dean Dalton received a broken finger after smashing into Petty.

D. Allison (above) won the pole with a speed of 107.785 mph, while Yarborough averaged 64.533 mph in a race slowed by three cautions for 28 laps. Yarborough won by more than a lap.

Volunteer 500
· · · · ·
July 14, 1974

*C*ale Yarborough rubbed fenders with Buddy Baker on the last lap and won again in the No. 11 Junior Johnson-prepared Chevrolet. Baker, in the No. 15 Bud Moore Ford finished second.

Baker had taken the lead on lap 454 and appeared on his way to victory when J.D. McDuffie's engine went up in smoke, bringing out the ninth caution. The green waved with two laps remaining. Yarborough drove under Baker coming off the second turn on the last lap. The cars rubbed and banged together in the third and fourth turns, and Yarborough came out the winner.

Richard Petty was third in a Dodge, Charlie Glotzbach fourth in a Ford, and Bobby Allison fifth in a Chevy. Only 10 of 30 cars finished the race, which ran under the yellow flag for over a fifth of its distance (105 laps). Petty won the pole at 107.351 mph, and Yarborough averaged 75.430 mph.

Johnson was pleased with Yarborough's win for an obvious reason: He had assumed ownership of the car from Richard Howard and was able to celebrate his first victory in that capacity since 1970.

Southeastern 500

· · · · ·

March 16, 1975

*R*ichard Petty (above with Lennie Pond) just kept on going, finally finishing six laps ahead of the field to post his second win at Bristol.

Driving the No. 43 Petty Enterprises/STP Dodge, Petty took the lead for the first time on lap 156 and led through lap 210. He also led laps 283-340 and the final 130 circuits. A totally tired Benny Parsons finished second in a Chevrolet, Buddy Baker was third in a Ford, Cecil Gordon fourth in a Chevy, and James Hylton fifth in another Chevy.

"I was just plain wore out. I couldn't take it anymore," Parsons admitted.

Completing the top 10 were Darrell Waltrip (relieved by Dick Brooks), David Sisco, Dave Marcis, Richard Childress and Ricky Rudd.

Baker won the pole at 110.951 mph and led the first 71 laps. Petty averaged 97.053 mph. There were two cautions for 27 laps.

Just 23 teams showed up to run the race, and of those 14 finished the race. Petty took the checkered flag in 2 hours, 43 minutes and 53 seconds and won $7,350.

Volunteer 500

· · · · ·

November 2, 1975

*T*o avoid the summer heat, NASCAR changed the date of the second race to November rather than July. Richard Petty won his 13th race of the season in the No. 43 Petty Enterprises/ STP Dodge. Lennie Pond took second in the Ronnie Elder No. 54 Chevrolet.

Darrell Waltrip was third, in the No. 88 DiGard Chevrolet. Dave Marcis drove his No. 71 K& K Insurance Dodge to fourth place, and Benny Parsons was fifth in the No. 72 L.G. DeWitt Chevy. Parsons wasn't up to snuff and called on "local hero" John A. Utsman (above) to drive relief and finish the race.

Completing the top 10 were Dick Brooks, Coo Coo Marlin, Cecil Gordon, James Hylton and Bruce Hill.

Cale Yarborough started from the pole after qualifying at 110.162 mph. He led three times for 172 laps. But for the 14th times in the last 25 races, he was sidelined by a blown engine.

By the mid-1970s, many drivers were easily identified by their cars' color schemes and sponsor decals and logos. (Above) "Petty blue," "STP red" and "43" all meant about the same thing.

(Left) Before Gatorade came along, Darrell Waltrip and the No. 88 DiGard Racing Co. Chevrolet were sponsored by Terminal Transport, a trucking company owned by the driver's father-in-law.

(Below left) The bright red Dodge driven by Dave Marcis full time in 1975 and '76 was owned by K&K Insurance Co. boss Nord Krauskopf.

(Below) One of the era's true "independents" –
drivers who ran with very little financial backing –
was Nashville, Tenn.'s David Sisco, who got into
this scrape with the No. 46 Dodge of Travis Tiller
when the engine in his No. 05 Chevrolet blew up in
March 1976. Sisco's Winston Cup career was relatively short – 133 races from 1971 through 1977 –
but he had his fans in Tennessee and elsewhere.

The "ancestor" of today's
NASCAR Busch Series, Grand
National Division, was the old Late
Model Sportsman circuit, which
gave some drivers a career boost
into Winston Cup racing and made
stars out of others. Jack Ingram
(11) of Asheville, N.C., won the
Sportsman championship in 1973-
74. When the series was
modernized in 1982, Ingram took
the title a third time, and he cor-
ralled it again in 1985. Darrell
Waltrip (88) never won an LMS
championship, but he won 13
races from 1982-89, including one
at Bristol in 1985.

Harry Gant was an outstanding
Late Model Sportsman competitor
long before he went into Winston
Cup Series competition more or less full time in
1979. After he took the checkered flag in the
Thunder Valley 300 at Bristol in May 1976, a tire
on his car shredded on the cool-down lap. Gant
drove into victory lane so his crew could put
fresh rubber on his winning car!

Southeastern 400
· · · · ·
March 14, 1976

*I*t turned into another fine run for Cale Yarborough (above with Roger Hamby), who seemed to atone for a winless 1975 "season" at Bristol. He drove the Junior Johnson Chevrolet to more than a one-lap victory over Darrell Waltrip, in the No. 88 DiGard Racing Co. Chevrolet.

Benny Parsons was third, also in a Chevrolet, while Dave Marcis was fourth in a Dodge, and Bobby Allison took fifth in Roger Penske's Mercury. Completing the top 10 were Dick Brooks, in a Ford; James Hylton, in a Chevrolet; Ed Negre, in a Chevrolet; Buddy Arrington, Plymouth; and J.D. McDuffie, Chevrolet.

Yarborough got around Waltrip's car on the 183rd lap and led the rest of the way. He was in a car that he drove into a crash earlier in the year at Richmond, Va., and he noted that the Johnson-led crew rebuilt it so well that it "handled as good as it ever has."

Buddy Baker won the pole at 110.720 mph, and Yarborough averaged 87.377 mph for the race.

There were six cautions for 79 laps, and four were brought out because of spinouts by Virginia driver Travis Tiller, who eventually dropped out with a blown engine. Yarborough said he was "real careful" when he passed Tiller's No. 46 Dodge.

Volunteer 400
· · · · ·
August 29, 1976

*S*peedway officials chopped 100 laps off the race, making it a 400-lap event. That and threatening weather left the grandstands half empty as only 12,000 people showed up to watch Cale Yarborough drive his Junior Johnson Chevrolet to a convincing victory.

Yarborough won by more than two laps over Dodge-driving Richard Petty. Darrell Waltrip and Benny Parsons, both in Chevrolets, finished third and fourth, respectively, while Buddy Baker was fifth in a Bud Moore Ford.

Yarborough averaged 99.175 mph in the race. Waltrip notched the pole at 110.300 mph and led the first 27 laps, but he was black-flagged for running over an air hose and fell out of contention.

(Far left) Walter Ballard (30) a journeyman driver from Houston, Texas, but based in Charlotte tries to hold off Dave Marcis (71) as Buddy Baker makes the pass during the 1976 spring event at Bristol. Baker started from the pole but didn't finish, while the win went to Cale Yarborough.

(Left) Bobby Allison (left) and Richard Petty were fierce competitors in the 1970s and rarely gave each other much slack on the track. They, however, respected each other and had a good relationship off it.

(Below) Track president Larry Carrier (right) congratulates Yarborough for another victory at his track. Miss Winston, Bebop Hobel helps with the winner's hardware.

THE DEAL IS IN THE WORKS

(Opposite page) Speedway owners Lanny Hester (left) and Gary Baker join Dale Earnhardt in victory lane on April 1, 1979 after Earnhardt won the Southeastern 500. It was the Kannapolis, N.C., racer's first NASCAR Winston Cup Series victory en route to an incredible career. The photograph is one of Baker's favorites.

(Left) Bobby Allison entered his own No.12 AMC Matador in the 1977 Volunteer 500. He qualified seventh fastest in a 29-car field but dropped out on the 16th lap with a broken clutch.

The tall lanky frame, moving under a baseball cap turned backward, rushed through the swinging doors of a lounge in downtown Bristol and announced: "Kick back the rug, big mama. Turn up the music, little cuzin. We gonna have Sad'ay night racin'!

"That guy Baker's done went and changed that summer racin' date from Sunday afternoon to Sad'ay night. The town will bust at the seams there will be so many people. Order lots more chicken and a heap more to drink. We gonna have us a crowd!"

The enthusiastic NASCAR stock car racing fan was right. So was Gary Baker when he made the move, in 1978, to switch the track's second of two annual Winston Cup races from the oppressive heat of Sunday afternoon to the relatively pleasant temperatures of Saturday night. He owned half the speedway at the time.

Baker grew up in Nashville, and became a certified public accountant (CPA) and attorney specializing in tax law.

His clients have included country music greats Johnny and June (Carter) Cash, Waylon Jennings; Conway Twitty (now deceased), Mel Tillis and a host of other top performers. Baker developed an interest in motorsports in the 1970s and gravitated toward sports cars and road racing. He competed in the 24 Hours of Daytona six times. He also drove a G.C. Spencer-prepared Chevrolet in the 1980 Winston 500 at Talladega. He started 15th and finished 20th, falling by the wayside after 145 laps with a broken oil pump. Based in Jonesborough, Tenn., Grover Clifton Spencer was something of a local hero. His career as a Winston Cup driver/team owner spanned the years 1958-77. Though he never won, he collected 138 top-10 finishes in 416 starts, including finishing second seven times.

During his high school days, Baker met classmate Lanny Hester, who later became a business partner. As an adult, Hester became a jewelry merchant and wholesaler and also, with Baker, owned a chain of kidney dialysis clinics.

"The performance aspects of racing always intrigued, me but I was equally fascinated by the business side of it, too," Baker recalled. "So when the opportunity came along to buy half of Bristol Speedway, I jumped at it. I'd never seen the track, but we made the deal over the telephone. Lanny was dabbling with racing like I was. So it was natural that when he heard about Bristol being for sale, he called and asked, 'Do you want to do this?' I told him, 'Yes, the deal is in the works.' "

It was the winter of 1977 when the two bought the track, and the purchase of Nashville Speedway, another stop on the Winston Cup circuit, followed in 1979. At the end of the second year (1980) Hester took the clinics down one road and Baker steered the race tracks down another.

"We operated through 1980 and 1981, and at the time the handwriting was on the wall at Bristol concerning the future of NASCAR racing," Baker said. "The fans loved it and were willing to buy tickets to see races."

At this point, the two had dumped a considerable amount of money into improvements. "We found it definitely needed work," Baker said. "During races the water supply would shut down. When we 'dug up' the problem, we found the entire track was being supplied by just one two-inch line, not nearly enough to take care of 25 or 30 thousand people. We fixed the problem.

"By this time there was something happening in racing. There were two phenomena – ticket scalping and counterfeit tickets. I remember telling state troopers that if

David Pearson (left) and Richard Petty (right) were on top of their game in the mid-1970s, while Darrell Waltrip was just beginning to show promise as a future star, challenging the two older drivers. During their careers, Pearson won five times at Bristol, while Petty scored a trio of first-place finishes. The all-time victory leader, though, is Waltrip, with 12 wins.

"But the biggest move I ever made was moving the August race from Sunday afternoons to Saturday nights. That took the speedway to the point where you really couldn't get a ticket." — Gary Baker

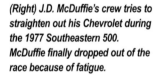

(Right) J.D. McDuffie's crew tries to straighten out his Chevrolet during the 1977 Southeastern 500. McDuffie finally dropped out of the race because of fatigue.

(Far right) Cale Yarborough's pit crew goes to work on his No. 11 Junior Johnson Chevrolet during the 1977 Volunteer 400. The final 34 laps were run under caution because of rain, and Yarborough won the race.

people didn't have race tickets, not to let them on the grounds. There was no way we could accommodate them, and that was at a time when 25 to 30 percent of our race tickets were actually sold on race day. So as fast as we could build the seats, people would buy them.

"But the biggest move I ever made was moving the August race from Sunday afternoons to Saturday nights. That took the speedway to the point where you really couldn't get a ticket. So many people said to us that we could not run Winston Cup races at night, but we had several reasons to switch. For one thing, night racing was more comfortable for the fans; two, it was more comfortable for the drivers; three, you had a built-in rain date. We had a second day to get a race in if we needed it. We saw

real quick that all we had to do was keep building seats and the fans would keep coming."

The fairgrounds track at Nashville, according to Baker, was an entirely different animal. In 1980 he purchased 700 acres (and was "closing in" on 300 more) to build a new superspeedway in the Nashville area. He then found a second 3,000-acre parcel that was, he said, "perfect." Unlike a lot of "bottom-line" types, Baker was something of a visionary, and he had fabulous plans for the future. The location was near an airport, rail service was available, it was accessible by ferryboat from Opryland and major highways ran north and south near the site. What more could you ask for? This was going to take big-time stock car racing to the next level.

(Top) Janet Guthrie, a pioneering female NASCAR driver of the 1970s, had to get out of her No. 68 Kelly Girl Chevrolet during an extremely hot 1977 Southeastern 500 and turn the car over to Rick Newsom, who drove to an 11th-place finish. Benny Parsons, Bobby Allison, Richard Childress and David Sisco also needed relief-driving help.

(Above) Savannah, Ga., driver Sam Sommers (27) charges underneath the Guthrie car on his way to a 15th-place finish in the M.C. Anderson Chevrolet. Anderson owned a construction company based in Savannah.

(Left) Action during the June 1977 Thunder Valley 300 Late Model Sportsman event. Morgan Shepherd (7) and Dale Earnhardt (8) race by Gene Glover's spinning car.

Southeastern 500
· · · · ·
April 17, 1977

Cale Yarborough, in the Junior Johnson Chevrolet, appeared to have the only key to victory circle at Bristol, and it seemed he didn't want to give it up (above). He breezed to his third straight victory at the track, this time winning by more than seven laps over the No. 90 Junie Donlavey Ford driven by Dick Brooks.

Yarborough, who was fighting the flu, proved just how tough he was by winning the pole with a speed of 110.168 mph and leading all but five of the event's 500 laps. Richard Petty finished third in a Dodge, followed by Neil Bonnett, also in a Dodge, and Benny Parsons in a Chevrolet.

While it was nowhere near hot at the track, Yarborough's "superman" reputation was further enhanced when five drivers needed relief and another, J.D. McDuffie, dropped out because of fatigue. Parsons was relieved by David Pearson; Bobby Allison by Ed Negre; Richard Childress by Elmo Langley; Janet Guthrie by Rick Newsom and David Sisco by Jerry Sisco.

Yarborough averaged 100.989 mph for the race, which took 2 hours, 38 minutes and 20 seconds to complete and won $23,300.

Volunteer 400
· · · · ·
August 28, 1977

Not even the rain could stop Cale Yarborough. He made it four straight victories at Bristol, winning over Darrell Waltrip. Benny Parsons was third. The first three drove Chevrolets. Dick Brooks was fourth in a Ford, and Tighe Scott finished fifth in a Chevy.

Yarborough took the lead for good with 66 laps to go. It rained, and the last 34 laps were run under caution due to the wet conditions. This prompted an outcry from Waltrip, who said that NASCAR's decision to finish the race under the yellow flag "cheated the fans out of the best finish here in a long time."

Janet Guthrie, the first female driver to race at Bristol, finished sixth in her second race at the track, although she needed relief-driving help from John A. Utsman, in her No. 68 Kelly Girl Chevrolet. Parsons, too, needed relief in another Bristol race, and this time he called on the services of Dave Marcis.

Yarborough started from the pole. He qualified at 109.746 mph and averaged 79.726 mph in the race. Crashes eliminated Richard Petty's No. 43 Dodge and the No. 52 Chevrolet of Jimmy Means.

The winning car, owned by Junior Johnson, failed pre-race technical inspection for the second time in three races. Johnson was fined $500 for having another illegal fuel tank in the car.

Johnson said he had no idea how the tank got into the car and told reporters to ask Herb Nab, the team's crew chief. Nab blamed chasis specialist Bobby Jones, sho said he installed the tank but was "just following instructions."

"During races the water supply would shut down. When we 'dug up' the problem, we found the entire track was being supplied by just one two-inch line, not nearly enough to take care of 25 or 30 thousand people. We fixed the problem." — Gary Baker

"Man, what did I get myself into?" It wasn't too long after Lanny Hester (right) took control of Bristol Raceway that he found there was more to being a track owner than greeting fans and drivers at the gate and having fun in victory lane. He personally had to supervise construction and repair projects that came with owner- ship, as the track needed some work. Hester ended up selling out to Baker.

"It was a beautiful setting," Baker said. "Today, it would be THE track on the NASCAR circuit – and we had a governor who was chomping at the bit to do something such as this. Everything was in place, but I guess, partially, anyway, I was intimidated by the size of the project."

In January of 1981, Hester sold his stock to Baker, who then took in two other partners, C.S. Baker (his father) and Stanley King. But in October of that same year, Baker bought them out and became the track's sole owner.

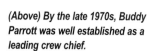

(Above) By the late 1970s, Buddy Parrott was well established as a leading crew chief.

(Top Right) Benny Parsons (72) takes the high line around Neil Bonnett in the 1978 Southeastern 500. Bonnett lasted 44 laps and then crashed his Jim Stacy Dodge out of the race. Parsons finished second in the L.G. DeWitt Chevrolet but needed relief from John A. Utsman.

(Right) We don't know who Donnie Allison's got on the stopwatch here, but he is caught up in the moment!

(Above) There was plenty of "action in April" during the 1978 Southeastern 500. Eventual race winner Darrell Waltrip (88) leaves Neil Bonnett (5); Roland Wlodyka (98); Lennie Pond (54); and Cale Yarborough (11) in his wake.

(Far left) Lanny Hester (left) gets a little advice from his partner, Baker, before trying his hand in a Dash Series race in June 1978.

(Above left) NASCAR's "stop-and-go" man hustles to avoid Tighe Scott's spinning Chevrolet (30) while Frank Warren motors past in his Dodge during the 1978 Volunteer 500.

(Left) Cecil Gordon's crew labors to fix his No. 24 Chevrolet during the '78 Southeastern 500.

(Below) While Gordon was in the pits, Dave Marcis (2), Benny Parsons (72), Skip Manning (92) and Darrell Waltrip were busy racing each other.

Southeastern 500
· · · · ·
April 2, 1978

*D*arrell Waltrip finally put his name in the win column here and won the "first" race at the newly renamed Bristol International Raceway. It was also the first win at the track for the driver of the No. 88 DiGard/Gatorade Chevrolet.

Waltrip went to the front with 102 laps go and held on to the lead, winning by more than a lap. He avoided a possible disaster early on when he was involved in a lap-45 accident that crunched in his car's left-front fender. Waltrip pitted, and quick work by his Buddy Parrott-led team got him back onto the track without losing a lap.

"The crew deserves the credit for this win," Waltrip said. "They did everything right today."

Chevrolet was 1-2-3 with Benny Parsons second and Dave Marcis third. Cale Yarborough was fourth in an Oldsmobile, and Lennie Pond fifth in another Chevy.

Neil Bonnett won the pole with a speed of 110.409 mph in the No.5 Jim Stacy Dodge (above). Waltrip averaged 92.401 mph.

The race also marked the debut of Richard Petty's 17-year-old son, Kyle, as an official Petty Enterprises crew member. The younger Petty went over the wall as a tire carrier, but his day ended at 47 laps when his dad crashed the No. 43 Dodge.

Volunteer 500
· · · · ·
August 26, 1978

*C*ale Yarborough, in a Junior Johnson-prepared Oldsmobile rather than a Chevrolet, led 327 of the 500 laps to win again at Bristol. He finished better than half a lap ahead of Benny Parsons, driving another Oldsmobile. Darrell Waltrip was third in a Chevrolet. Dick Brooks was fourth in a Ford, and Richard Petty rounded out the top five in a Chevrolet. It was the "King's" second race in a Chevy, as he'd decided to end a long association with Chrysler Corp. products.

Finishing sixth through 10th were Dave Marcis (Chevrolet), Richard Childress (Oldsmobile), J.D. McDuffie (Chevrolet), D.K. Ulrich (Chevrolet) and Roger Hamby (Chevrolet).

Lennie Pond (above) won the pole in an Olds. He turned the track at 110.958 mph, while Yarborough averaged 88.628 mph in the race, which took 3 hours and 25 minutes to complete, and won $15,910.

Pond, as it turned out, figured prominently in the race. Early on, he tangled twice with Waltrip and again with Cecil Gordon in an accident that saw his Harry Ranier-owned No. 54 Oldsmobile on top of the wall on the frontstretch. He finally parked the car and went on to fill in for Petty, who was still sore from an accident at Michigan the previous week.

(Left) Richard Petty (43) goes side by side with D.K. Ulrich (40) in the 1978 Volunteer 500. Ulrich was one of the era's most enduring "independent" driver/car owners.

(Below far left) Petty dices with the damaged No. 48 Chevrolet of James Hylton. They finished fifth and 17th, respectively, in the '78 Volunteer 500.

(Below left) Hylton finds himself sandwiched between the Chevrolets of Jimmy Means (52) and Nelson Oswald. All three owned the teams they drove for.

(Below) The DiGard Racing Co. crew swarms over the No. 88 Gatorade Chevrolet during a practice session. Darrell Waltrip started second and finished third, a lap down.

(Left) Ferrel Harris (8) started eighth, in a Chevrolet owned by noted race car fabricator and bodyman Robert Gee of North Carolina, in the 1978 Volunteer 500. Even after running into a suspension problem (inset), he still managed to complete 425 laps and finish 18th. Neil Bonnett (5) wasn't as lucky. He dropped out when the engine in his Osterlund Racing Chevrolet blew up on lap 288.

One day when he was sizing up his next move, Baker got a telephone call from Ralph Seagraves, R.J. Reynolds' Special Events Operations boss. Seagraves told Baker that he would be receiving a call from a guy named Warner Hodgdon – a California businessman who kept increasing his presence in NASCAR racing – and that he should take the call. Because Baker thought that Seagraves walked on water, he did just that.

Warner W. Hodgdon of San Bernardino, Calif., was the owner of the National Engineering Co. and a major developer of the City of Industry (a planned, incorporated nonresidential community for business and industry 30 miles east of Los Angeles founded in 1957). In April 1982 he bought 50 percent of Bristol speedway and a half-interest in the accompanying drag strip. By the end of the year, he also purchased half of the fairgrounds track in Nashville, which was also Baker's.

"Somehow it made sense to me to get Warner involved in the Nashville project. He owned National Engineering and was developer of the City of Industry. So I sold him 50 percent of the Nashville and Bristol speedways. With his construction experience it was totally logical, so that is how that got to the table," explained Baker.

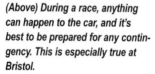

(Above) During a race, anything can happen to the car, and it's best to be prepared for any contingency. This is especially true at Bristol.

(Above right) In the 1979 Southeastern 500, Benny Parsons (27), Bobby Allison (15) and Cale Yarborough all drove for well sponsored race teams. Valleydale Meats was a local meatpacker and retailer; Warner Hodgdon would briefly become the track's owner; Anheuser-Busch was just beginning to deepen its involvement in the sport.

(Right) Buddy Baker waits while his Ranier Racing Chevrolet is serviced during the '79 Southeastern 500. Later, he and Yarborough made contact and both crashed out of the race.

In April 1982, Warner W. Hodgdon of San Bernardino, Calif., the owner of the National Engineering Co. and a major developer of the City of Industry, bought 50 percent of Bristol speedway and a half-interest in the accompanying drag strip.

A lot of fans who were at Bristol on April 1, 1979 will remember the time as the day Dale Earnhardt won his first NASCAR Winston Cup Series race. Cale Yarborough (11) and Buddy Baker, however, might have a different recollection of the event. Baker won the pole in the Spectra-sponsored, Harry Ranier-owned Chevrolet and led the first 138 laps. Yarborough started fifth in the Junior Johnson Oldsmobile and led just one lap. Then on lap 216, as they were trying to pass a slower car, Baker hooked Yarborough and into the wall they went. Yarborough's teammates tried their best to repair the car and get their man back into action. The effort, however, was for naught.

"**B**ristol had an extremely brilliant future. You just kept adding to it and there was practically no debt load. Bristol could finance its own growth, but Nashville was a different story." — **Gary Baker**

Bobby Allison (left) and Buddy Baker enjoyed varying degrees of success at Bristol. Baker captured the pole for three races at the track, while Allison started on the pole twice and won four races. Both drivers' careers ended in 1988.

"Bristol had an extremely brilliant future. You just kept adding to it and there was practically no debt load. Bristol could finance its own growth, but Nashville was a different story. That was the only difference Warner and I had. I wanted to build a state-of-the-art superspeedway on 3,000 acres, and Warner had some concept for Nashville about expanding the present facility."

In existence as an auto racing track since 1904, Nashville is one of the oldest continuously operating speedways in the country. Originally a one-mile dirt oval, by the time NASCAR showed up there in 1958 it had been paved and reconfigured into a half-mile race course. It underwent several changes over the years, and when Geoffrey Bodine won the last Winston Cup race there – the July 14, 1984 Pepsi 420 – it had become a 0.596-mile layout with an accompanying quarter-mile track facing the covered grandstand.

Why did NASCAR take Nashville off the Winston Cup Series schedule? Times were beginning to change again, and with it the circuit itself. Its series sponsor, R.J. Reynolds Tobacco Co., had put a lot more money into the pot for the 1985 season and had added "The Winston," a special non-points event that featured big money for the the winner. With a maximum capacity of about 20,000 people, the series had simply outgrown the Nashville track.

The start of something big! When Dale Earnhardt arrived at Bristol International Raceway for the 1979 Southeastern 500, he was a short-track "hero" back home in North Carolina, with just 15 Winston Cup races under his belt. He was still basically unknown - or known better as "Ralph Earnhardt's son"— in NASCAR circles. That all changed, though, when the young charger took the lead in the April 1 event for the final time with just 25 laps left and beat Bobby Allison to the checkered flag by three seconds. Darrell Waltrip, in the No. 88 DiGard/Gatorade Chevrolet finished third. Earnhardt's first big-time victory was also the first for his Osterlund Racing team. "I'll probably believe this in the morning," the 28 year old driver said. Earnhardt would go on to win the Winston Cup championship seven times and become a nationally known sports star.

(Above) Three faces of the 1970s: Ricky Rudd (left) ran his first Winston Cup race in 1975 and went on to become one of the circuit's most successful drivers. D.K. Ulrich (center) and J.D. McDuffie were two of the circuit's staunchest "independents" - owner/drivers, who operated with limited budgets. Ulrich sold his team in the mid-1990s and McDuffie died in a racing accident in 1991.

(Below) Terry Labonte (44) has to keep an eye on James Hylton (48) while attempting to pass Benny Parsons during the 1979 Volunteer 500.

"Nashville was small, old and landlocked and had a fair board that had no clue as to what NASCAR racing could do for the Middle Tennessee area," Baker said. In fact, the fair board was antagonistic toward racing. I heard where some of the people on the board actually thought the fairgrounds would be better off without the track. So I thought it was time to go, but Warner was adamant about expanding the place."

Their problems grew. When Baker took on Hodgdon as a partner, to keep things amicable, they added a "put-call" option in their agreement. That meant that one partner could name a price and offer to buy the other one out, as long as the partnership lasted at least a year. When the two men realized they couldn't agree on the future of racing in Nashville, Baker asked Hodgdon to let him buy his 50 percent. Hodgdon, however, had an option

of "flipping it around" and buying Baker's 50 percent at Baker's price. So, in short order – mid-1983 – Baker owned zero percent of both tracks, and Hodgdon owned all the stock in both.

In effect, the man who had bought the golden goose had to watch it fly away!

"I was one sick puppy, and I still am today," Baker said in early 2001. "For seven or eight years after that I would not listen to a Bristol race on the radio or watch one on television. I have yet to go back there. (Baker did, indeed, return to the track in April 2001 as the owner of a NASCAR Busch Series car raced by his son, Brad, 26. He marveled at all the changes that had taken place and said he was glad he'd come back.) That was the 'call' of the put-call. It's mandatory that when you exercise it, the other partner has to see or buy. I asked Warner to please sell it back to me, but he had the right to flip the table. Had I refused, he could have taken me to court."

Baker, however, didn't exit the world of auto racing promotion totally destitute. When he and Hester purchased Bristol, they gave Carrier and Moore "less than $1 million." After his hand was forced by Hodgdon, he left the table with "approximately $2 million."

Southeastern 500
· · · · ·
April 1, 1979

*F*ans will talk about this one for years to come. Dale Earnhardt posted his first NASCAR Winston Cup Series victory on this fair day. It was his 16th start on the major league circuit.

The second-generation driver from Kannapolis, N.C., was driving a Chevrolet owned by Rod Osterlund and Jake Elder was his crew chief. Earnhardt led 164 laps. He took the lead for the final time with 25 laps to go and outran Bobby Allison, who was in the No. 15 Bud Moore Ford, by three seconds.

"I'll probably believe it in the morning," said the 28-year-old Earnhardt. This is a bigger thrill than my first-ever racing victory.

"This was a win in the big leagues - the Grand Nationals. It was against top caliber drivers. It wasn't some dirt track back home."

Darrell Waltrip finished third in a Chevrolet, Richard Petty was fourth, two laps down, in an Oldsmobile, and Benny Parsons finished fifth, three laps back, also in an Olds.

Buddy Baker started from the pole. He qualified at 111.668 mph but crashed out on lap 216 after tangling with Cale Yarborough. Earnhardt, who started ninth, completed the race in 2 hours, 55 minutes and 39 seconds, averaged 91.033 mph and won $19,800. There were six cautions for 44 laps.

Volunteer 500
· · · · ·
August 25, 1979

*R*ichard Petty won his first pole in two years, but Darrell Waltrip came from a lap behind in the final 40 laps to win the race.

It appeared Benny Parsons might win. He passed Dave Marcis on lap 395 to take the lead and was in front 20 laps from the end when he and Richard Childress wrecked. Waltrip and Petty pitted and caught up, ready for the green. It waved 14 laps from the finish, and Waltrip won by a few car lengths.

"I don't know what happened," said Parsons. "I was going around Childress, and the next thing I knew I was in the grass."

Both Waltrip and Petty were driving Chevrolets. Bobby Allison finished third in a Ford. Parsons was fourth in a Chevy, and Cale Yarborough fifth in a Chevy. Joe Millikan finished sixth, David Pearson was seventh, Terry Labonte, eighth, Ricky Rudd, ninth and Bill Elliott, 10th.

Pearson was substituting for Dale Earnhardt, who had been sidelined by injuries he received in a wreck at Pocono, Pa., at the end of July. In this event, Pearson got out of the car and turned it over to relief driver Lennie Pond.

Petty ran 120.524 to capture the pole. Waltrip averaged 91.493 to win the race. Six cautions for 60 laps slowed the pace.

(Above) Mid-pack runners like Joe Millikan (72), Tommy Gale (64) and Dave Marcis often staged their own "race within a race" as they did here during the 1979 Volunteer 500.

(Right) Cale Yarborough (11) takes the low groove in passing Millikan. Yarborough started fourth and finished fifth in the '79 Volunteer 500.

(Far right) Darrell Waltrip came from a lap behind late in the '79 Volunteer 500 and, driving a car he called "Bertha," landed in victory lane.

So in 1983, Hodgdon became the sole owner of Bristol and Nashville speedways. Because of extensive business problems in California, late in 1984, Hodgdon, who had made a huge, albeit brief, splash in NASCAR racing, was forced to admit he was having money problems and was the target of lawsuits equaling millions filed against him. On February 8, 1985, Bristol Speedway and accompanying drag strip went on the auction block. The Bank of Virginia said that Hodgdon and his National Raceways, Inc., failed to make December's $102,000 mortgage payment. Larry Carrier, who sold the track in 1978 and became its president and general manager in 1983 under Hodgdon, assumed the role of the track's trustee, appointed by a federal bankruptcy judge in California. Hodgdon then filed bankruptcy in Tennessee.

In January of 1986, Carrier purchased the facility from the bank and announced that he had "paid everyone off" and was now the "sole owner of both the speedway at Bristol and the drag strip."

So during his all-too-brief time at the helm of the "good ship Bristol," Baker did steer it on a proper course. When, however, he came upon an unexpected storm and ran aground, it was the end of another chapter in the story of the track in Thunder Valley. ∎

(Above) After a crash at Pocono, Pa., earlier in the season sidelined Dale Earnhardt, David Pearson filled in for him in the Osterlund Racing Chevrolet. At the 1979 Volunteer 500, Pearson needed relief help from Lennie Pond, who brought the car home seventh.

(Left) Ricky Rudd was seven laps down at the finish of the '79 Volunteer 500 but still finished ninth in the No. 90 Junie Donlavey Chevrolet.

(Far left) En route to another Winston Cup championship in 1979, Richard Petty was enjoying himself. Here track owner Gary Baker presents Petty with the pole winner's trophy.

(Left) Dave Marcis started eighth and was running second late in the race when an incident with a lapped car knocked him back to 18th at the finish.

(Above) In the late 1970s you could still "rough it" in the "cheap seats" at Bristol! For a few bucks you could sit on the grass and enjoy the race.

(Right) Here, Dave Marcis looks like he's ready to return to his native Wisconsin for a bit of hunting or fishing!

(Far right) One thing's always been the same, though, and that's the drama that unfolds in the pits. Over the years, pit stops have gotten faster, but the basic drill hasn't changed that much.

(Above left) "Say cheese!" Dale Earnhardt turns the tables on a photographer.

(Above right) In a Winston Cup Series driving career that spanned the years 1972-81, Richard Childress was also an accomplished all-around mechanic and engine man.

(Left) Childress (3), here running with Earnhardt in 1980, never won a Winston Cup race but was always competitive. His racing career changed when he hired Earnhardt as his driver in 1981 and then brought him onto the team for keeps in 1984.

Valleydale Southeastern 500
· · · · ·
March 30, 1980

*D*ale Earnhardt came straight from a victory at Atlanta to take the victory at Bristol. It was his second straight win in the spring race, and his third in a blossoming Winston Cup Series career. Driving the No. 2 Rod Osterlund Chevrolet, Earnhardt led the final 135 laps and was one-half lap ahead of runner-up Darrell Waltrip, in the No. 88 DiGard Chevrolet at the finish.

Bobby Allison was third in the No. 25 Bud Moore Ford, the last driver to run the full 500 laps. Then came Benny Parsons and Cale Yarborough, both in Chevys, while Joe Millikan, Harry Gant, Richard Petty, Dave Marcis and Terry Labonte completed the top 10. Rookie of the year candidate Jody Ridley, survived a spin (above) to finish 11th in No. 90 Junie Donlavey Ford.

Earnhardt was, to say the least, jubilant over the victory. He said when he joined his team he figured it would take a year to win a race. But with his victory in this event last year, and another one in this race ...

"I don't see any reason why I can't win the Grand National championship this year," he said.

Yarborough won the pole at a speed of 111.688 mph. Earnhardt averaged 96.977 mph in the race, slowed three times for 14 laps under the yellow.

The race also marked the first time the track had secured an event sponsor. The relationship between BIR and Valleydale, a Tennessee meatpacker and retailer, would last through the 1991 season.

Busch Volunteer 500
· · · · ·
August 23, 1980

*T*he engine in James Hylton's Chevrolet blew up on lap 486, bringing out the caution and setting the stage for a dramatic 10-lap dash to the checkered flag among Cale Yarborough, Dale Earnhardt and Darrell Waltrip. That was also exactly the order of finish.

Yarborough, who had taken the lead from Waltrip on lap 478, led to the finish in the No. 11 Busch-sponsored Chevrolet. Earnhardt pulled alongside Yarborough but had to back off to avoid hitting Roger Hamby's No. 17 Chevrolet, which was 35 laps down. That killed his chance of winning a third consecutive race at Bristol. They drove under the checkered flag 1-2-3 with Yarborough in front, Earnhardt on his bumper, and Waltrip third. STP-sponsored Richard Petty was a lap down in fourth place, and Benny Parsons was fifth. All five drivers were in Chevrolets.

"I think I would have had him (Yarborough) if it hadn't been for the 17 car," Earnhardt said.

Bobby Allison (Ford), Dave Marcis (Chevrolet), Lennie Pond (Oldsmobile), Richard Childress (Chevrolet) and D.K. Ulrich (Chevrolet) completed the top 10. "Independent" driver Cecil Gordon kept his No. 24 in the running for awhile but finished 19th.

Yarborough won the pole with a speed of 110.990 mph, and he averaged 86.973 mph in a race slowed by caution flags 10 times for 57 laps.

(Top) Members of the media were afforded a bird's-eye view of the entire speedway from the first-turn press box, which opened in the late 1970's. The sport's increasing popularity stimulated increased coverage in newspapers and magazines, as well as television.

(Above) Harry Gant (47) avoided trouble when Terry Labonte spun out and crashed during the 1980 Busch Volunteer 500. The engine in Gant's Race Hill Farm Chevrolet later blew up, and he finished 14th.

(Right) In an era when motorcycle jumpers were commonplace, Jimmy "The Flying Greek" Kourfas had a real gimmick – he jumped a school bus, ramp-to-ramp, over a row of motorcycles! The Greek was part of the pre-race entertainment for the 1980 Busch Volunteer 500 on Aug. 23, but there was just one glitch: He successfully made the jump, but the bus gouged out the track when it landed. The start of the race was briefly delayed until the asphalt was patched.

(Right) When Tim Richmond showed up in NASCAR Winston Cup racing in 1980 it didn't take long for that year's Indianapolis 500 top rookie to pick up a new nickname – "Hollywood."

(Far right) The 1981 season was the first of six Darrell Waltrip ran for the No. 11 team of Junior Johnson. At Bristol, the new combination went right to the front of the field.

(Above) The Valleydale 500 victory was Waltrip's third in just six starts in '81.

(Above right) Petty vs. Petty! In this event, Kyle Petty (42) managed to upstage "Daddy." He finished 11th, while Richard ended up 29th because of engine failure.

(Right) Richmond drove D.K. Ulrich's No. 99 UNO-sponsored Buick to a 10th-place finish. UNO was a popular card game of the era.

(Left) Harry Gant was a NASCAR Late Model Sportsman standout until he joined the Winston Cup circuit full time in 1979. In '81, he hooked up with the Skoal-sponsored Mach One team owned by Hollywood celebrities Hal Needham and Burt Reynolds. In that year's August Busch 500, he finished 11th at Bristol in the No. 33 "Skoal Bandit" Pontiac.

(Bottom left) Benny Parsons (15) ran into a bit of a problem in the '81 Valleydale 500 but still finished fifth. Avoiding Parsons' mishap are Ricky Rudd (88) and Joe Millikan.

(Below) Kyle Petty qualified a Petty Enterprises Buick 11th fastest for the '81 Busch 500. His race ended in the 29th lap because of a broken transmission.

(Top) Team owner Harry Ranier began the 1981 Winston Cup Series season with Bobby Allison as his driver and an engine additive for a sponsor. By the time the Busch 500 rolled around in August, that sponsor had departed and Ranier got Hardee's restaurants to back him for the rest of the year.

(Above) Joe Ruttman (2) gets neighborly with Richard Petty in the August '81 Busch 500. Like Petty, Ruttman was sidelined with mechanical trouble.

(Right) Allison seems to be enjoying the company of one of his young fans. He finished fourth in the '81 Busch 500.

Valleydale 500
· · · · ·
March 29, 1981

*D*arrell Waltrip, after several controversial seasons with the DiGard Racing Co., raced like a new man in 1981. In this event, he drove to an easy victory, providing team owner Junior Johnson his eighth win in the last 14 races on this 0.533-mile high-banked oval.

It was also the new combination's third win in the season's first six races.

Waltrip, in a Mountain Dew-sponsored Buick, finished a straightaway ahead of Ricky Rudd, who was in Waltrip's old ride, the No. 88 DiGard/Gatorade Oldsmobile. Bobby Allison was third in a Pontiac. Morgan Shepherd, also in a Pontiac and was fourth. Benny Parsons was fifth in the No. 15 Bud Moore Ford – despite spinning out three times – and the top four drivers were on the same lap.

Dale Earnhardt was leading on lap 118. Waltrip bumped him, causing him to wreck and he finished 28th. Earnhardt later drove relief for Terry Labonte and brought the No. 44 Billy Hagan-owned Buick home seventh, five laps down.

"It was a situation where there was a lot of tight traffic. Darrell should have backed off. He ran into me," Earnhardt said of his incident with the race winner.

Waltrip won the pole with a speed of 112.125 mph and averaged 89.530 mph in the race. He completed it in 2 hours, 58 minutes and 36 seconds in front of 33,000 fans and won $22,450.

Busch 500
· · · · ·
August 22, 1981

*D*arrell Waltrip made it his year at Bristol. The winner of the spring race, he also triumphed in the summer event, as well.

Driving a Buick, Waltrip went to the front on six occasions, led all but two of the final 198 laps and was more than a lap ahead of Ricky Rudd when the caution came out. The race finished under the yellow. Rudd was in, the No. 88 DiGard/Gatorade Chevrolet. Terry Labonte finished third in a Buick, and Bobby Allison and rookie driver Ron Bouchard, also in Buicks, were fourth and fifth, respectively.

Waltrip also closed to within 50 points of leader Allison in the race for the 1981 Winston Cup Series championship. The driver from Franklin, Tenn., compared the Junior Johnson organization to a stick-and-ball team that was "peaking just at the right time."

Benny Parsons finished sixth, in the Bud Moore Ford; Lake Speed and Tim Richmond were sixth and seventh, both in Oldsmobiles, while Dave Marcis and Buddy Arrington rounded out the top 10, in Buick and Dodge, respectively.

Defending champion Dale Earnhardt, was the victim of bad luck again when he crashed on the 32nd lap and finished 27th.

Waltrip won the pole at 110.818 mph and averaged 84.723 mph in the race.

(Above) Action in the 1982 Valleydale 500: Terry Labonte (44) drove for Billy Hagan but was sponsored by J.D. Stacy, who owned the No. 2 Buick driven by Joe Ruttman. Bobby Allison was in his first season in the No. 88 DiGard/Gatorade Chevrolet, while Richard Petty was going after his 196th Winston Cup victory.

(Right) "Fits like a glove, right?" Geoff Bodine tries on Tim Richmond's full-face helmet prior to the start of the May 1983 Valleydale 500. The design had been adopted by open-wheel drivers but was till fairly new in NASCAR stock car racing.

(Top) On May 22, 1982, Bristol hosted a special event for the Late Models of the American Speed Association (ASA), an Indiana-based organization. The field included Davey Allison, Darrell Waltrip and Rusty Wallace. The race was won by Mike Eddy.

(Top left) Robert "Boobie" Harrington played a key role in the J.D. Stacy racing organization in the early 1980s, as a mechanic, manager and crew chief.

(Above) The Stacy crew makes a tire change on the No. 28 Ranier Racing Pontiac, driven by Buddy Baker, during the 1982 Busch 500. Baker started fifth and finished ninth.

(Left) Darrell Waltrip (11) fends off Dale Earnhardt and Ronnie Thomas (25) during the '82 Busch 500. Waltrip won the race, Earnhardt was sixth and Thomas lasted only 30 laps before something broke on his car.

Valleydale 500
· · · · ·
March 14, 1982

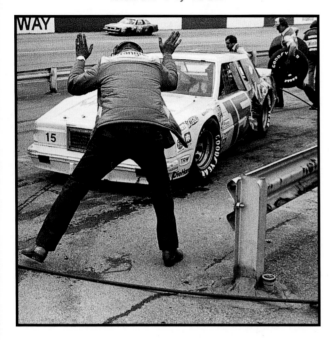

*D*ale Earnhardt, driving the No. 15 Bud Moore-owned Ford, was out front, leading Darrell Waltrip by 12 seconds. Earnhardt had taken the lead on lap 286 and appeared to be a shoo-in winner.

Then Bristol being Bristol, Gary Balough, in the No. 75 Rahmoc Racing Buick, spun in front of him on lap 398 of 500 and Earnhardt tangled with the loose metal. As Earnhardt made an emergency pit stop for repairs (above), Waltrip came breezing by in his No. 11 Mountain Dew Buick and, never headed, drove to victory, giving team owner Junior Johnson his 15th win on the 0.533-mile track in the last 22 races.

Waltrip beat a recovering Earnhardt to the finish line by a straightaway. Morgan Shepherd was third in the No. 98 Benfield Racing Buick. Terry Labonte finished fourth in the Billy Hagan Chevrolet, a lap down, followed by Bobby Allison in the DiGard Chevrolet, two laps behind the winner.

Twenty-one of the 30 starting cars finished, and there were just three cautions for 25 laps.

Waltrip started on the pole after qualifying at 111.068 mph. He averaged 94.025 mph in the race and won $26,520.

Busch 500
· · · · ·
August 28, 1982

*T*wenty laps from the finish, Darrell Waltrip took the lead and drove the No. 11 Junior Johnson/Mountain Dew Buick to victory – Johnson's 16th in the last 23 races here.

Waltrip took the lead during the final caution, brought out when Terry Labonte and Dave Marcis tangled. Labonte was leading the race when he ducked into the pits for a quick fuel stop. He got back onto the track and Marcis drove into him.

When that happened, the yellow flag flew, and most of the field made a mad dash for the pits. The driver of the pace car hesitated in going onto the track – the cars not in the pits were still running fast - and when the pace car did go onto the speedway, Waltrip passed it and then was picked up as the leader. While some observers wondered if Waltrip was actually a lap down, several scorers had him completing an extra lap.

Bobby Allison in a Chevrolet was second, Harry Gant in a Buick was next, followed by Labonte in a Buick and Morgan Shepherd was fifth in yet another Buick.

Tim Richmond (above) won the pole with a speed of 112.507 mph. Waltrip averaged 94.318 in the race and collected $22,925.

(Top left) NASCAR Busch Series star driver Jack Ingram celebrates in Bristol's victory lane after winning the 1982 Pet Dairy 150.

(Middle left) Broadcaster and former Winston Cup champion Ned Jarrett (right) decided to join car owner Junior Johnson (center) and driver Darrell Waltrip in victory lane after Waltrip won the 1982 Busch 500.

(Top right) Gary Nelson got his start in Winston Cup racing in the early '80s as crew chief for the DiGard Racing Co. team. Today, he's the NASCAR Winston Cup Series director – the circuit's "chief enforcer!"

(Left) Sam Ard (00) and Phil Parsons run side by side during the August 1983 Free Service 150 Busch Series race at Bristol. Parsons captured the pole and Ard won the race.

(Left) Bristol has, over they years, played host to all sorts of motorized competition - including the Tri-Cities Bobtail 200 Great American Truck Racing special event on Sept. 18, 1982. (Inset) Bob Lashlee (right) and his crew chief, Virgil Earp, smile after being awarded the trophy for winning the competitive event.

SEATS PAID FOR THEMSELVES

(Left) Kirk Shelmerdine, Dale Earnhardt's crew chief, heads back toward the pit wall after completing a tire change during the 1985 Valleydale 500. Earnhardt started the race 12th, led most of the laps and won the race.

(Opposite page) Sharon and Warner Hodgdon were true partners in every aspect of their marriage. When Warner began increasing his interest in racing – which included purchasing the Bristol track – Sharon was right at his side. Although his involvement in NASCAR racing was relatively brief, its impact was deep. Financial problems outside of the sport forced him to leave it.

The year escapes him – it was probably in the mid to late 1970s – but Warner W. Hodgdon said the first driver he ever sponsored in a NASCAR Winston Cup circuit race was Donnie Allison. The event was held at the now long-gone Ontario (Calif.) Motor Speedway, which was not too far from Hodgdon's hometown of San Bernardino. Ontario was a 2.5-mile showplace that unfortunately never made much money. It opened in 1970 with a USAC-sanctioned Indy Car race, and shortly after Benny Parsons won the Los Angeles Times 500 Winston Cup Series season-ender on Nov. 15, 1980 it closed and was then leveled.

Hodgdon's name shone brightly in NASCAR racing for just a relatively few years, but the man did have a sizeable impact on the sport. He backed drivers and teams, sponsored Winston Cup and what are now Busch Series races, controlled all or parts of five race tracks and for a while owned 50 percent of one of the most powerful race teams ever to compete in the Winston Cup Series. His involvement in racing began in 1977 when he was part of a group that built the first aluminum stock-block, normally-aspirated engine for Indy Car racing. It was based on an American Motors Corp. Matador engine, and because Bobby Allison, Donnie's older brother, was running the Matador in NASCAR, Hodgdon somehow got to meet the Winston Cup superstar.

Hodgdon was a wealthy "racing sportsman" who made much of his fortune in real estate, industrial and business development and with his own company, National Engineering. He also came in and revitalized the City of Industry in California. It was also Hodgdon's involvement in this enterprise that would eventually force his departure from racing.

Hodgdon was a wealthy "racing sportsman" who made much of his fortune in real estate, industrial and business development and with his own company, National Engineering.

(Top) Ricky Rudd's hopes for a victory in the 1983 Busch 500 went up in a shower of sparks when a rear suspension part broke on his Richard Childress Racing Chevrolet. Rudd did finish the rain-shortened event, which was won by Darrell Waltrip.

(Above) Bill Elliott (9) tries his best to keep from being "eaten up" by Dale Earnhardt (3) and Tommy Ellis in the 1984 Valleydale 500. Elliott finished ninth, Earnhardt was seventh and Ellis ended up 28th when the brakes on his Morgan-McClure Racing Chevrolet failed. The race was won by Darrell Waltrip.

In 1979, Bobby Allison was driving the No. 15 Bud Moore Engineering Ford, which was in need of a sponsor. Hodgdon stepped in, put his name on the car and his involvement in Winston Cup racing began to snowball. Hodgdon also sponsored Moore in 1980, and he got his friend, Mike Curb, to back the team, too. Curb, the one-time lieutenant governor of California, who owns Curb Records, would go on to form his own Winston Cup and Busch Series teams.

Although Hodgdon doesn't put it exactly like this, perhaps if he hadn't agreed to help a fellow Californian, Rod Osterlund, the late Dale Earnhardt may have not won his first Winston Cup championship in 1980. Earnhardt, a young short-track charger from Kannapolis, N.C., joined the new Osterlund Racing team in 1979 and went on to win the rookie of the year award. Top rookie honors, however, didn't mean much as far as money was concerned, and when the team arrived at Riverside (Calif.) International Raceway in January for the first race of the 1980 season, it was in trouble.

"Roland Wlodyka (Osterlund team manager) came to me in the garage and said his team didn't have enough money to leave the race track," Hodgdon recalled. "So I picked up the tab. It was $3,000 a month and they also charged their tires to me. They were having a rough time, but that's how I became close to Dale. And Mike Curb was running for governor that year, so we put his name on Rod's cars along with mine. Strangely enough, I met Rod just one time. It was at the last race of the year at Ontario."

Through Allison, Hodgdon struck up an acquaintance with Neil Bonnett, another Alabama-based driver – and a protégé of Allison's. A friendship developed, which was fortunate for Bonnett, who was "between rides" in early 1979. Hodgdon, who wanted to see if Bonnett had possibilities as an open-wheel racer, brought him to Indianapolis Motor Speedway for a test run. While at Indy, Bonnett received a phone call from someone with one of the most well known of all Winston Cup teams, Wood Brothers Racing. The Woods had fired their longtime driver, David Pearson, following a pit-road foul-up in the spring race at Darlington, S.C., and wanted to know if Bonnett would take his place for the rest of the year. Hodgdon agreed that Bonnett's future lay in Winston Cup racing and the Indy Car experiment was scrapped.

Bonnett ended up racing for the Wood Brothers 17 times in 1979 and right through the 1982 season. When the Woods' longtime sponsor, Purolator, decided to get out of racing, Hodgdon and his National Engineering Co. assumed team sponsorship duties in August 1981.

Valleydale 500
• • • • •
May 21, 1983

When you're hot, you're hot – and Darrell Waltrip was one hot driver. He drove the Johnson-Hodgdon Chevrolet to his seventh victory at Bristol. It was his 15th win in the last 20 Winston Cup Series short-track races.

Waltrip led 288 laps, including the final 94 and won by a straightaway over Bobby Allison, who was driving the DiGard Buick. Although it was just the 11th race of the year, it seemed a battle between Waltrip and Allison for the NASCAR Winston Cup championship was already shaping up. At least there was a "psychological" fight, as Allison had recently said Waltrip had opened his mouth too wide and parted with owner Junior Johnson's (above right) secrets.

"I guess this goes to show you we haven't given away all our secrets," Waltrip said after his win.

Morgan Shepherd, also in a Buick, was third. Neil Bonnett was fourth in a Chevrolet and Richard Petty fifth in a Pontiac. The top 10 was rounded out by Terry Labonte, Ron Bouchard, Bill Elliott, Dale Earnhardt and Tim Richmond.

Earnhardt led 116 of the first 158 laps but failed to make a scheduled pit stop for fuel and ran out of gas. That cost him and he finished five laps down.

Bonnett started from the pole after qualifying at 110.409 mph. Waltrip averaged 93.445 for the race. Because of just four caution flags for 22 laps, the race took less than three hours.

Busch 500
• • • • •
August 27, 1983

Darrell Waltrip, behind the wheel of the powerhouse Johnson-Hodgdon Buick seemingly is almost an unbeatable force at Bristol. This time around, he beat Dale Earnhardt out of the pits on the final pit stop and was in front when rain ended the race after 419 of the scheduled 500 laps had been completed.

Earnhardt led for 73 laps and the yellow waved when Neil Bonnett wrecked. Both Earnhardt and Waltrip pitted for four tires. Junior Johnson's crew got Waltrip out first. The Bud Moore crew had trouble changing the left-rear tire on Earnhardt's Ford. The race finished under caution with Bobby Allison, Geoff Bodine and Terry Labonte rounding out the top five.

After Waltrip found out he knocked 20 points off Allison's lead, he said he thought his outfit was in "pretty good shape to take our third straight championship."

Rounding out the top 10 were Harry Gant, Ron Bouchard, Morgan Shepherd, Richard Petty and Neil Bonnett.

Waltrip averaged 89.430 mph and completed the event in 2 hours, 29 minutes and 50 seconds. Joe Ruttman captured the pole with a speed of 111.923, but he failed to lead a lap and finished 18th, 40 laps down.

Valleydale 500
· · · ·
April 1, 1984

*M*ake it eight straight victories for team owner Junior Johnson at Bristol International Raceway and seven consecutive trips to victory lane for his driver, Darrell Waltrip on the 0.533-mile high-banked oval.

This time, Waltrip, in the No. 11 Budweiser Chevrolet, took the lead on lap 457 and used Bobby Allison's misfortune to grab the victory. Allison, in the No. 22 DiGard Buick, had the field covered and had lapped Waltrip when his car developed rear end problems. The defending Winston Cup Series champion lost 25 laps in the pits and finished 19th. Waltrip, meanwhile, edged Terry Labonte's No. 44 Chevrolet at the finish line by two seconds. Ron Bouchard was third in a Buick, followed by Dave Marcis in a Pontiac and Tim Richmond, also in a Pontiac.

"This," said Waltrip of his Bristol resume, "is really incredible. With that kind of record, the credit has to go to somebody other than the driver."

Rounding out finishing spots sixth through 10 were: Ricky Rudd, in a Ford; Dale Earnhardt, in a Chevrolet; Richard Petty, in a Pontiac; Bill Elliott, in a Ford, and Joe Ruttman, in a Chevrolet.

Rudd, who won the pole at 111.390 mph in the No. 15 Bud Moore Ford, was two laps down. Waltrip averaged 93.967 mph, finished the event in 2 hours, 50 minutes and 10 seconds and won $31,670.

Busch 500
· · · ·
August 25, 1984

*T*erry Labonte beat and banged his way to the front as though he were back on a Texas short track. He survived two wrecks to win his first race at Bristol which also put him first in Winston Cup points – and helped pave the way towards the 1984 series championship.

It was just such a night. There were 12 caution periods for 66 laps. Labonte was involved in a four-car wreck early in the race when he and Dale Earnhardt banged fenders. Later on in the event, Labonte and Neil Bonnett tangled, putting Bonnett out of the race.

Finally, Labonte took the lead from Geoff Bodine on lap 377 and drove on to victory in the Billy Hagan Chevrolet. Bobby Allison finished second in a Buick. Dick Brooks was third in a Ford, two laps down, followed by Dave Marcis in a Pontiac and Harry Gant in a Chevrolet.

Completing the top 10 were: Bill Elliott (Ford); Mike Alexander (Oldsmobile); Sterling Marlin (Oldsmobile) Greg Sacks (Chevrolet) and Earnhardt (Chevrolet). Bodine ended up finishing 22nd when the rear end in his Hendrick Motorsports Chevrolet broke on the 396th lap.

Bodine won the pole at 111.734 mph. Labonte averaged 85.365 mph for the race, finished it in 3 hours, 17 minutes and 19 seconds and won $28,480.

"In fact, I was the first one ... or one of the first ones ... I believe ... to give a driver a contract," Hodgdon said. "I paid Neil $80,000 a year plus 50 percent of the winnings."

Bonnett and Hodgdon left the Wood Brothers at the end of '82 to spend one season driving for and sponsoring the Rahmoc Racing team. Then in 1984, Bonnett signed on to drive a "second car" for the famed Junior Johnson team of Ingle Hollow, N.C. That arrangement worked perfectly because in November 1982 Hodgdon had purchased half of Johnson's team, which made it Johnson-Hodgdon Racing.

"In fact, I was the first one ... or one of the first ones ... I believe ... to give a driver a contract," Hodgdon said. "I paid Neil $80,000 a year plus 50 percent of the winnings. I paid him that, win, lose or draw. And then we'd pay him extra for testing and things like that because I thought Neil was great. He could have been the best, just like Dale." In all, Bonnett recorded 156 top-10 finishes, including 18 victories in 363 starts. After several racing injuries, he retired at

the end of 1989. After deciding to make a comeback, he was killed while practicing for the 1994 Daytona 500.

By then Hodgdon was deeply immersed in the sport. In April 1982 he purchased a 50-percent interest in the speedways in Bristol and Nashville, Tenn., becoming Gary Baker's equal partner. As 1982 drew to a close, he also owned half of North Wilkesboro (N.C.) Speedway, half of Richmond (Va.) Fairgrounds Speedway, and a majority of the stock in Phoenix (Ariz.) International Raceway. In addition to having Bonnett under contract, his team sponsorships, and owning half of the Junior Johnson operation, he also sponsored Winston Cup races at North Carolina Motor Speedway in Rockingham and NASCAR-sanctioned events on the West Coast.

The pipe fitter who went racing: Neil Bonnett was a plumber by trade who drove in his first Winston Cup event in 1974. By the late '70s he was "under the wing" of Warner Hodgdon, who thought Bonnett had a lot of potential and advanced the driver's career. Before losing his life in a racing accident in 1994, Bonnett won 18 Winston Cup races in 363 starts – but none at Bristol.

"It didn't take me long to figure that this thing (NASCAR Winston Cup racing) was going to go some-place with television," Hodgdon said. "The promoters were concerned that TV would hurt ticket sales, but I looked at it the opposite way. I thought TV had exposed so many people that the tracks wouldn't have enough seats. I mean that's why people advertise on TV in the first place. Anyhow, I knew Bill France Sr. and got along with him very well, as well as Ralph Seagraves and some other people at R.J. Reynolds."

It was Seagraves who hooked him up with Bristol's Gary Baker. After the sale, Hodgdon said he felt like he'd also became a partner with Reynolds, which he called a "good company."

"Every time I bought (into) a track, I'd fly down to Florida to see Bill France Sr. and Jr.," Hodgdon said. I told them, 'I don't want you to think I'm being competitive with NASCAR. I just like the sport; I think it's really going places and I want to participate.' A lot of people were struggling financially at the time, but I was fortunate to be hitting good times. Each time I bought one, I'd tell the France's exactly what I was paying. I told them if they wanted to buy them, I'd sell at the same price. They never took me up, but they couldn't say I didn't ask them."

(Left) Buddy Arrington checks out his Dodge's engine before the start of the 1984 Valleydale 500. He started 24th and finished 22nd, completing 464 laps.

(Below left) Terry Labonte (44), as he prepares to pass Neil Bonnett (12) and Greg Sacks (51) enroute to winning the 1984 Busch 500. The victory played a big role in Labonte notching the Winston Cup championship that year.

(Below) Waltrip's crew chief, Jeff Hammond, checks in with the boss before the start of the '84 Busch 500. Today, both are racing analysts for Fox TV's Winston Cup Series broadcasts.

When it came to his disagreement with Baker that led to his becoming the sole owner of the Bristol and Nashville tracks, Hodgdon said that Baker's version of the story was basically true. The split came because they didn't agree about keeping Nashville International Raceway versus building a new superspeedway.

"I think the Nashville track could have been made a little bit larger, and you could have gotten more seats in it by working with the city," he said. "I saw the Nashville track kind of like I looked at the Bristol track, and Bristol, I think, has now got about 150,000 seats. I basically said, 'Why invest in something 2.5 miles long when you can sell about just as many tickets at a half mile?' It would have taken a much smaller investment, so that was it."

Hodgdon's influence on NASCAR-sanctioned racing is even a bit deeper than is chronicled here. Suffice it to say, however, his "reign" in the sport was all too brief. In early 1984, the scuttlebutt was that he was having fiscal problems on both coasts, and by the end of the year rumor had become fact. Hodgdon was in deep financial trouble.

Valleydale 500
· · · · ·
April 6, 1985

*I*t's a fact of life: Some race wins come easy and some hard. This one came hard for Dale Earnhardt – NASCAR Winston Cup racing's "one tough customer."

About 100 laps into the 500-lap event the power steering box failed on Earnhardt's Richard Childress-owned Wrangler-sponsored Chevrolet. For the rest of the race, Earnhardt wrestled with the car and battled with Ricky Rudd. With 18 laps to go, Earnhardt took the lead from Rudd and beat him to the finish line by a nose. Rudd was in the Bud Moore Ford. Terry Labonte was third in a Chevrolet, Buddy Baker was fourth in an Oldsmobile, and Rusty Wallace rounded out the top five in Cliff Stewart's Pontiac.

"I've never driven a car which had lost the power steering," Earnhardt said. "I hope I never have to again.

"I had to pull on the steering wheel so much my right arm went to sleep."

Although there were 14 caution flags for 90 laps, 20 of the 30 starting drivers drove under the checkered flag. Kyle Petty finished sixth, in a Ford; Lake Speed was seventh in a Pontiac; Richard Petty, eighth, in a Pontiac; Bobby Hillin Jr., ninth, in a Chevrolet and Ken Schrader, 10th in a Ford.

Harry Gant won the pole at 112.778 mph. Earnhardt averaged 81.790 mph, completed the event in 3 hours, 15 minutes and 42 seconds and won $31,525.

Busch 500
· · · · ·
August 24, 1985

*W*ith 18 laps to go, Dale Earnhardt knocked Tim Richmond's Blue Max Racing Pontiac out of the groove, took the lead and drove to victory in the Richard Childress-owned Chevrolet.

Earnhardt led 343 of the 500 laps, but found himself in second place with 40 laps to go. Also, he had lost the lead to Richmond by pitting too early under the caution flag. About 10 miles from the finish, Earnhardt bumped him and made what turned out to be the winning pass. Richmond finished second in a Pontiac, the "Double Thunder" team of Neil Bonnett and Darrell Waltrip was third and fourth in Chevrolets and Bill Elliott fifth in a Ford.

"He (Earnhardt) used one of his normal tactics, but I'm not mad," Richmond said. "It was good, hard racing, and I knew what to expect from him."

Harry Gant, Ron Bouchard, Richard Petty, Ricky Rudd and Lake Speed filled in finishing spots six through 10, and 21 of the 31 starting cars finished the race.

Earnhardt won the pole with a qualifying speed of 113.586 mph. He averaged 81.388 in the race. There were 11 caution flags for 82 laps.

What happened? While it's been a long time, Hodgdon is still sensitive about the subject. Perhaps that's understandable. In short, he and his wife, Sharon, looked up one day and saw their investment in the City of Industry and his company, National Engineering, crumbling before their eyes. In the spring of 1984, someone high up in the Hodgdon business organization was implicated in a bid-rigging scandal, and National Engineering was sued for $33 million.

In September, Hodgdon had to give up his interest in North Wilkesboro, and two months later North Carolina Motor Speedway sued him for $100,000 for "overdue" sponsorship money. This led Johnson to get Hodgdon's 50 percent of the race team back, and finally two lawsuits totaling $53 million forced Hodgdon into bankruptcy. Hodgdon's mistake, it turned out, was that he never incorporated National Engineering. That meant that he and his wife were personally responsible for the misdeeds of an "unfaithful employee." When his California base collapsed, his racing investments had nothing to stand on.

"I had an unfortunate situation because of some employees who worked for me, and it looked like it could get really serious" he said. "Everything my wife and I had was in our names, and it fell right to the pillow. So I had to let everything go because I was a partner with everybody. Whether it was the North Wilkesboro people, Junior Johnson, Richmond ... although I owned 100 percent of Bristol, I felt like I was a partner of Larry Carrier because I still owed him money. I didn't know how it was going to shake out, so I just backed off and let everything go.

"But I felt I started a momentum in NASCAR when things were down. I felt, hopefully, we were a positive influence in the sport, and I loved everybody in it. So the best thing to do was back off and not let them get sucked in with me. It took a long time, but I came out unscathed as far as any culpability was concerned. I really got hurt financially, but I'm sure everybody I had anything to do with in NASCAR came out to the better."

(Top) April 6, 1985 – the Valleydale 500 – was not a good day for Darrell Waltrip and his Budweiser Chevrolet. After Waltrip was caught up in some on-track action, his crew made repairs and put him back in the race. He later exited with engine failure. Sterling Marlin was having a decent day in the No. 95 Sadler Brothers Chevrolet until he was sidelined by an accident. (Above) Team owner Raymond Beadle (left) and his driver, Tim Richmond, talk strategy before the '85 Valleydale 500. Richmond, the victim of a crash, was the first driver out of the race. (Left) Ricky Rudd (15) and Dale Earnhardt swapped rides for the 1984 season. Rudd left the Richard Childress Chevrolet for Bud Moore's Ford, while Earnhardt ended his association with Moore to join Childress. Wrangler was caught in the middle and sponsored both teams that year!

Hodgdon hasn't, after a decade and a half, totally rid himself of the "racing bug." He said he has plans to build a race car shop in Indianapolis that would house an Indy Racing League (IRL) team. While he would not become a team owner – just a landlord – he feels that the IRL has the same potential for success NASCAR did 20 years ago. Also, because Indianapolis Motor Speedway now hosts three big events (Brickyard 400, Indy 500 and a Formula One race), Indy is the place to be "before they flip the lid on your casket."

"At the economic level I bought into NASCAR, it was like buying in for nothing. But that was 15, 16 years ago," Hodgdon said. "I paid $150,000 for half of Richmond, and I think I read where Paul Sawyer sold it for $220 million. I think I bought Bristol (oval track) and the drag strip for a million and a half. Now Larry's sold it to Bruton Smith for $28 million. All the seats Larry put in paid for themselves."

And to sum up his ownership of Bristol ...?

"We kicked the horse in the butt, but we just didn't cross the finish line!" ■

(Right) The "Brew Boys" of 1985. Neil Bonnett (left), Bobby Allison (center) and Bill Elliott had one thing in common before the start of the Valleydale 500 – bright red uniforms!

(Bottom left) "Battle of the Beers": Darrell Waltrip (11) and Bobby Allison go at it during the '85 Valleydale 500. Allison finished 13th, 13 laps off the pace, while Waltrip's Junior Johnson Chevrolet succumbed to engine failure on the 179th circuit.

(Below) Bobby Hillin, quickest in second-round qualifying for the 1986 Valleydale Meats 500. received a Busch Pole award from Ned Jarrett.

(Left) Ralph Seagraves (right), here with David Pearson (left) and Cale Yarborough, played a significant role in the history of what's now known as Bristol Motor Speedway. The R.J. Reynolds special events boss, who passed away in 1998, brought Gary Baker and Warner Hodgdon together and was an influential member of the racing industry.

(Middle left) "Doggone it!" Richard Petty checks out the damage to his Curb Motorsports/STP Pontiac after an incident in the 1984 Busch 500. Somehow, Petty managed to finish the race.

(Below left) Warner Hodgdon (here with NASCAR flagman the late Harold Kinder) made a lot of friends in racing. He said he was glad his problems in the sport left most of them unaffected.

(Below) Bill Elliott keeps his battered Ford out in front of Terry Labonte (44) and Darrell Waltrip (11) during the 1985 Valleydale 500. Elliott finished 11th in the race.

ASPHALT WASN'T WORKING

(Opposite page) Larry Carrier probably thought his involvement with Bristol Speedway was over after the sale to Gary Baker. Baker lost the track, however, to Warner Hodgdon in a business deal. Then when Hodgdon's bicoastal empire crumbled, Carrier found himself back at the helm of the track in late 1985.

(Left) The track – and its pit area – had changed quite a bit from the time Carrier sold the speedway and then took it over again. Compared to today, though, racing in the mid-1980s was a laid-back affair.

Larry Carrier took possession of the speedway for the second time in 1985, and he began to make major changes to upgrade the racing. The track underwent a radical facelift in 1992 – from asphalt to concrete. The track's surface kept deteriorating and Carrier, unable to find a suitable sealer, tore up the asphalt and replaced it with concrete. When you look at the concrete surface, think of the great pyramids in Egypt: Nobody knows how they were built, and Carrier's resurfacing project is still almost as big a mystery.

Larry Carrier's critics said concrete would not work, but the wily speedway owner and Bristol-area businessman disagreed. They scoffed when he said he was going to tear the asphalt off Bristol International Raceway and replace it with the aggregate-cement mix usually used to build a race track's walls. In short, Carrier made it work without the advice and expertise of a dozen or more civil engineers. You might say doing it his way was a "concrete" idea.

"The asphalt wasn't working, so I figured I didn't have a whole lot to lose by switching to concrete," Carrier said. "I had tried everything, including chips in the asphalt, and I had the best engineers in the country give me their opinions. Some of these people would come and say, 'Let me show you.' I tried three times with the asphalt. It would not work.

"The cars go too fast at Bristol for asphalt. The track is too steep for asphalt, and the cars are going so fast into the turns. I had spent more than $250,000 on asphalt. The cost of the concrete was about $100,000, and it is still there.

"When I got the idea for concrete, I went across town to a place where employees of Joe Loven's Kingsport construction company were laying a lot of concrete for the floor of a big wholesale building," Carrier recalled. "I went over my plans with the foreman and a couple more people. They said they could do the job, and it wasn't long until we began work at the speedway."

93

Full House! Adding a new seat to the grandstands was like planting a seed. It would "grow" into another race fan. Under Carrier's second stewardship, Bristol International Raceway would continue to grow in popularity as a prime place to enjoy NASCAR competition.

Carrier announced his resurfacing scheme six weeks after the running of the April 5 Food City 500. His mind was made up after he watched a team test tires for Goodyear and saw parts of the new asphalt surface come apart.

"I'm still not satisfied with the (track)," Carrier said. "By using every method known to man in connection with asphalt materials, plus the timing of our races, has made it impossible for our asphalt to cure. During our April races, we had the top of the asphalt track still stripping in places.

"The down-pressure at Bristol Raceway is unreal, and the asphalt has not held up in any of the last three times in which the track was resurfaced."

Jeff Byrd, vice president and general manager of the track today, said it is still a mystery how Carrier made the change from asphalt to concrete, noting "he used two-by-fours and seat-of-the-pants engineering and did the entire track. He did not shoot a single grade on it and it turned out great".

Construction workers ran cables through the concrete, all drawn up to 7,000 pounds pressure so the concrete would not contract or expand. Hence, it stays right there where it is and has traction from top to bottom and all the way around the oval.

Night Moves! There's something about a race under the lights that brings out a crowd – such as the one here for a Busch Series event in 1988. Bristol tickets for NASCAR's "Triple A" division are now also at a premium.

Valleydale 500
• • • • •
April 6, 1986

*I*t was a memorable afternoon for Russell William "Rusty" Wallace, who visited victory circle for the first time in Winston Cup competition. The win came in his 72nd series start.

"Some people doubted Rusty's ability," noted his Blue Max Racing crew chief, Barry Dodson. "Some people doubted he'd ever make it big.

"Well, he made it big today. Mark this date."

On this day he drove his No. 27 Pontiac to a straightaway victory over Ricky Rudd, who piloted a Ford. Darrell Waltrip was third and Harry Gant fourth, both in Chevrolets, while Bill Elliott was fifth in a Ford.

It may have been a great day for Wallace and his crew, but it rough on others. Accidents took out five drivers, among them Neil Bonnett, Dave Marcis and Ronnie Thomas, who was transported to a local hospital but was later released.

Wallace started 14th, took the lead for the first time on lap 240 and led the final 101 circuits. He averaged 89.747 mph despite seven cautions for 56 laps. Geoff Bodine won the pole at 114.850 mph but dropped out on lap 239 with engine failure.

Busch 500
• • • • •
August 23, 1986

*D*ale Earnhardt wrecked too early, and Darrell Waltrip, who started 10th, took the lead for good with 144 laps to go and recorded yet another win at Bristol for himself and team owner Junior Johnson.

Earnhardt, who was seriously pursuing a run toward the championship for himself and team owner Richard Childress, saw his points lead shrink a bit after he tried to move a lapped car out of the way and instead went into the wall himself. He did, however, manage to recover enough to finish fourth, one lap down.

After that happened, all Waltrip had to contend with was Terry Labonte and Geoff Bodine. In the No. 11 Budweiser Chevrolet, Waltrip beat Labonte to the checkered flag by a whopping 8.55 seconds to win for the 10th time at Bristol. Labonte was in the Billy Hagan Chevrolet. Geoff Bodine, in the Hendrick Motorsports Chevrolet, was third and Harry Gant fifth. Completing the top 10 finishers were Tim "Hollywood" Richmond, Richard Petty, Bobby Allison, Bobby Hillin Jr. and Alan Kulwicki.

Bodine won the pole with a speed of 114.665 mph. Waltrip averaged 86.934 mph in the race, and there were six caution periods for 56 laps. Waltrip completed the event in 3 hours, 3 minutes and 55 seconds in front of 35,000 spectators and won $41,725.

Byrd still laughs at the whole idea, but it's a laugh of wonderment instead of scorn. "It takes an army of engineers to build one of these flat tracks these days, but here is Larry with his two-by-fours and Joe Loven with his concrete trucks, and a bunch of workers out of Texas who were building that warehouse. Larry put the whole crowd together, and they built a heckuva speedway," Byrd said.

After the job was completed, it was time for a dress rehearsal of sorts. Three Winston Cup drivers – Davey Allison, Derrike Cope and Kyle Petty – showed up in early July to test the new surface. Next, about a week before the Aug. 28-29 Food City 250-Bud 500 weekend, about 25 Winston Cup and Busch Series teams participated in a "dress rehearsal" on the new concrete. Their opinions were mixed, but they, however, held no surprises for Carrier.

"We'd better eat our Wheaties, a characteristically terse Terry Labonte observed. "You're vibrating so much in the corners, it's difficult to see the car in front of you," Dale Jarrett noted. "We're all going to have to make appointments to see our dentists because if you have fillings, after the race they're not going to be there anymore."

Sterling Marlin called the new surface a "little rough" but "not unbearable" and said the only difference he noted was that his rear-view mirror vibrated a bit more than was normal. Morgan Shepherd, who was racing for the Wood Brothers, said he thought the track surface was rough but foresaw more side-by-side racing. "I love it. Once we run in the rubber I think it's going to be OK. I think we'll be running top to bottom once we get enough rubber down."

Darrell Waltrip, the track's most successful driver with 11 wins, was adamantly anti-concrete and didn't mind saying so.

"I don't like it. It's rough. It's worse than it's ever been," he said. "The straightaways are smooth, but the corners are washboardy.

"There are a lot of ripples that make the car chatter. It gives you a real insecure feeling."

Of course, when Waltrip returned and won the Bud 500 by trouncing the competition (he was almost 10 seconds in front of runner-up Dale Earnhardt), his comments were a bit more subdued. He said if the concrete was just smoothed out a bit, Bristol would be a "great place to race."

"I sort of figured what they might say," Carrier said. "And I hit the nail on the head. The first few drivers out said the track was too bumpy. I had a machine parked inside the track. It was a machine with diamond blades. We used it to cut off the humps, and we kept cutting until the surface was smooth."

> "**I** don't like it. It's rough. It's worse than it's ever been," he said. "The straightaways are smooth, but the corners are washboardy." — Darrell Waltrip

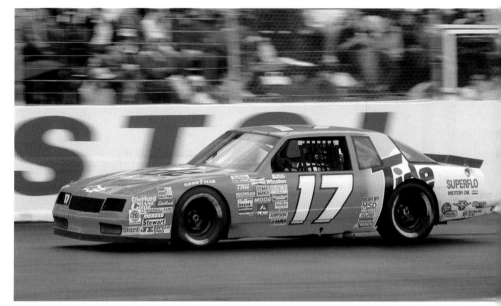

(Top) When this photo of Darrell Waltrip "at speed" was taken in 1987, he had already won 10 times at Bristol. The three-time champion was initially opposed to racing on a concrete surface – and then he won the first race on it!

(Above) "Pal, this is how you do it on a short track." Dale Earnhardt (left) seems to be giving Bill Elliott a bit of advice prior to the 1987 Valleydale Meats 500, which Earnhardt won. Maybe something clicked because Elliott returned to win the 1988 version of the event.

Valleydale Meats 500
· · · · ·
April 12, 1987

*D*efending Winston Cup champion Dale Earnhardt played offense in this race at Bristol. He hit a few and passed a few more, and he drove to victory for the third straight time in 1987.

On lap 252, the driver of the No. 3 Richard Childress Racing Chevrolet tapped race leader Sterling Marlin, sending him into the first-turn wall. During a red-flag period for rain, Earnhardt was warned by NASCAR about rough driving, but Earnhardt replied that you had to be "aggressive" to race on Bristol's high banks.

"He hit me from behind and spun me," Marlin said. "I'm the leader of the race. He's supposed to pass me, not spin me out."

On his way to victory, Earnhardt, who led all but one of the final 122 laps, beat Richard Petty to the checkered flag by less than a second. Earnhardt was in a Chevrolet and Petty in a Pontiac. Ricky Rudd was third, Bill Elliott fourth and Alan Kulwicki fifth, all in Fords.

The race was a long one – 3 hours, 31 minutes and 27 seconds – with 13 cautions for 125 laps. The attrition rate was high, with seven drivers eliminated by accidents and two more because of engine failure. Earnhardt averaged 75.621 mph and won $43,850. Harry Gant won the pole with a qualifying speed of 115.674 mph.

Busch 500
· · · · ·
August 22, 1987

*B*oth races in 1987 go to Dale Earnhardt, as he dominated the summer event in the Richard Childress-owned Chevrolet.

He took the lead on lap 57 and was in control the rest of the race. While other drivers did lead occasionally, the race basically belonged to the driver of the Wrangler Jeans No. 3, who took the lead for good on lap 349. Rusty Wallace finished second, 5.5 seconds behind Earnhardt, in a Pontiac. Ricky Rudd was third in a Ford, Terry Labonte fourth in Junior Johnson's Chevrolet and Richard Petty finished fifth in his company's STP Pontiac. He was the last driver to complete all 500 laps.

Completing the top 10 were Geoff Bodine (Chevrolet), Rick Wilson (Oldsmobile), Harry Gant (Chevrolet), Bill Elliott (Ford) and Neil Bonnett (Pontiac), who was relieved by Ken Schrader.

Labonte won the pole with a qualifying speed of 115.758 mph. Earnhardt averaged 90.373 mph for the race. There were eight caution periods for 49 laps. The winner went home with $47,175.

Valleydale Meats 500
. . . . .
April 10, 1988

*F*or a guy who cut his racing teeth on the bullrings of north Georgia, it was always sort of strange that Bill Elliott had never won a Winston Cup race on a short track.

That all came to an end when Elliott, a winner 22 times on superspeedways and once on a road course, posted his first short track win here on this spring day.

The driver of the No. 9 Melling Racing and Coors-sponsored Ford Thunderbird started 13th, ran up front and took the lead for the first time on lap 379. He stayed in the lead but toward the finish had Geoff Bodine and Mark Martin nipping at his rear bumper. Ten laps from the finish, Bodine's Hendrick Motorsports Chevrolet clipped Elliott's rear bumper, sending him into a complete spin-around.

When the caution came out, Bodine stayed on the track to take the lead, while Elliott and Martin pitted for tires. The race went green with five laps left, and Elliott took the lead for good with three laps to go, passing Bodine. Martin got by, too, for second place and finished a couple of car lengths behind Elliott. Rusty Wallace finished fourth behind Bodine, while fifth went to Bobby Allison.

Rick Wilson started from the pole (his first in the series) in an Oldsmobile, qualifying at 117.552 mph but spun out three times, crashed once and finished 25th. Elliott averaged 83.115 mph for the race and won $45,750. There were 12 cautions for 70 laps.

Busch 500
. . . . .
August 27, 1988

*E*n route to the 1988 Winston Cup championship, Bill Elliott was having quite a year. Included was his "historic" victory at Bristol in the spring and a close second here in the summer.

Dale Earnhardt slipped by Alan Kulwicki just nine laps from the finish and then held off Elliott in the final laps to win before 42,000 fans. Earnhardt, driving a Chevrolet, led 220 laps. Elliott was the only other driver on the lead lap at the finish. He was driving a Ford. Geoff Bodine, a lap down, finished third in a Chevrolet. Davey Allison, in a Ford, was fourth. Kulwicki, a Ford driver, finished fifth. They also completed all but one lap.

Rounding out the top 10 finishers were Harry Gant (Chevrolet); Darrell Waltrip (Chevrolet); Richard Petty (Pontiac); Rusty Wallace (Pontiac) and Bobby Hillin Jr. (Buick). The race was slowed 14 times for 83 laps, and crashes took out the cars of Brett Bodine, Dale Jarrett, Mark Martin, Rick Mast, Dave Marcis and Brad Noffsinger.

Kulwicki won the pole with a speed of 116.893 mph. Earnhardt averaged 78.775 mph. There were 14 caution periods for 83 laps.

The day before the race, Rusty Wallace was severely shaken when he crashed hard during a practice session. ESPN pit reporter, Jerry Punch, a medical doctor, was credited with reviving the driver, who spent the night in a hospital. He finished the race with relief help from Larry Pearson.

"You didn't have to work at being a promoter. You could just stand there, and

it would come to you. Racing had become a family sport by this time, and the

fans came to the track ... and so did the sponsors."   — Larry Carrier

Carrier, here with driver Tim Richmond, was able to enjoy himself a lot more the second time around as Bristol's owner and promoter. Life was easier in the respect that he didn't have to worry a lot about filling the track's grandstands.

Carrier said it was the single greatest moment of his life when he saw that the concrete did the job. "I finally decided I was going to do what I wanted to do, and I would have done it to begin with if I knew what I know now. I listened to too many people, I guess."

Carrier did well with the facility after buying it from the bank. "It was about this time that racing took off," he said. "You didn't have to work at being a promoter. You could just stand there, and it would come to you. Racing had become a family sport by this time, and the fans came to the track ... and so did the sponsors."

Through it all, Carl Moore has been a part of state government. From 1965 through 1969, he served in the Tennessee House of Representatives. Then he served in the state senate from 1976 until 1988. Since that time he has been in state government relations as a lobbyist.

"I think about it often," Moore said. "Right after we built the track, a local farmer threatened to sue us because he said all the noise made his cows quit giving milk."

Moore seems to wonder how many dollars he would have saved if the farmer had taken him to court and won.

Carrier kept the facility until January 1996 when he sold it to O. Bruton Smith's Speedway Motorsports, Inc. Carrier asked for $20 million after taxes, so Smith's purchase price was $25,280,000.

"I sold it because I had other things I wanted to get into," Carrier said. "I was running the International Hot Rod Association (IHRA), which I founded. I had about 70 drag strips and eight national meets. If I were doing it all over again, I would not do anything different."

For Larry Carrier, his introduction to motorsports was strictly a business investment. Racing then grew on him, and he became one of its biggest fans. ∎

Valleydale Meats 500
·····
April 9, 1989

Busch 500
·····
August 26, 1989

*D*id Rusty Wallace really win the Valleydale Meats 500? That could be the subject of an argument, as the race was slowed by a record 20 caution flags. At the conclusion of the race, there had been 98 laps run under the yellow flag.

Wallace and Darrell Waltrip squared off in a 15-lap duel in the sun after the final yellow, and Wallace won by less than a second. Geoff Bodine, who Wallace passed for the lead with 63 laps to go, finished third. Davey Allison was fourth and Dick Trickle fifth. Wallace drove a Pontiac. Waltrip and Bodine were in Chevrolets, Allison was in a Ford and Trickle in a Buick.

Most of the slowdowns were for wrecks, and members of the "crash-out" club were Phil Parsons; Morgan Shepherd; Bobby Hillin Jr.; Hut Stricklin; Ernie Irvan; Brett Bodine; Butch Miller and Ken Schrader. Greg Sacks led the race five times for 99 laps but ended up finishing seventh after scraping the wall and falling off the pace. Mark Martin ended up sixth, Ricky Rudd, eighth, Bill Elliott, ninth, and Harry Gant, 10th.

Wallace averaged 76.034 mph for the race, finished it in 3 hours, 30 minutes and 18 seconds and won $48,750. Martin won the pole at 120.278 mph. Attendance was listed as 43,000.

*P*op Singer Bob Seger had a hit with his tune, Night Moves, but it's doubtful Dale Earnhardt was humming it as he made his own "night move" and took himself out of contention for another Bristol victory.

Darrell Waltrip took over after Earnhardt spun in turn four, hit the wall and messed up the front of his Chevrolet. Earnhardt motored past Waltrip on lap 269 and held the lead through lap 294. Then something happened to the No. 3 Goodwrench Chevrolet, as it spun completely around in the fourth corner and just kissed the retaining wall. But that was enough to knock the front end out of alignment. Earnhardt continued on and struggled to a 14th-place finish, 10 laps down.

Waltrip led 239 of the 500 laps as 45,000 fans watched. He was driving a Hendrick Motorsports Chevrolet. Alan Kulwicki (above, left) finished second in a Ford over five seconds behind Waltrip. Ricky Rudd was third in a Buick, Harry Gant fourth in an Oldsmobile, and Terry Labonte fifth in Junior Johnson's Ford.

"We wanted to serve notice," Waltrip said in victory lane. "We didn't want to take any prisoners. We ran hard all night and didn't look back."

Rounding out the top 10 were Rusty Wallace, Bobby Hillin Jr., Jimmy Spencer, Neil Bonnett and Dale Jarrett.

Kulwicki won the pole at 117.043 mph. Waltrip averaged 85.554 mph for the race. There were 11 cautions for 69 laps.

Valleydale Meats 500
· · · · ·
April 8, 1990

*D*avey Allison overcame the disadvantage of pitting on the backstretch and then nipped Mark Martin in a photo finish to win the seventh race of his career. The finish was so close that NASCAR officials would not declare a winner until they studied the television replay.

Allison qualified his No. 28 Robert Yates Racing/Texaco Havoline Ford 19th, which meant he had to pit on the backstretch. He didn't take the lead until lap 392, but it fell into his lap when he didn't make a pit stop when the last of 13 caution flag periods (for 65 laps) began 109 laps from the finish. Allison later explained that because he had made a stop for new tires 30 laps before, there was no need to do so again. Darrell Waltrip mounted a challenge but dropped back with 25 laps left because of a flat tire and finished ninth.

Ricky Rudd was third in a Chevrolet. Terry Labonte finished fourth in an Oldsmobile, and Rick Wilson was fifth in a Pontiac. Ernie Irvan won the pole at 116.157 mph. Allison completed the event in 3 hours, 3 minutes and 15 seconds, averaged 87.258 mph and won $50,100. What made the win sweeter was the fact that he'd survived a fender-bending incident with the spinning car of rookie Rob Moroso on the 171st lap.

Busch 500
· · · · ·
August 25, 1990

*C*alifornia native Ernie Irvan scored the first Winston Cup victory of his career on this day, taking the lead from Dale Earnhardt with 90 laps left and then holding off Rusty Wallace by a whisker – 0.21-second.

It was also the first victory for the Kodak-sponsored Morgan-McClure Chevrolet team from nearby Abingdon, Va., as well as something of a vindication for team owner of record Larry McClure. He fired driver Phil Parsons after the third race of the 1990 season and replaced him with Irvan.

Earnhardt started from the pole and led 350 of the first 410 laps. Irvan passed Earnhardt with 90 laps to go. Then Wallace, a Pontiac driver, charged into second place. Mark Martin was third in a Ford, followed by Terry Labonte and Sterling Marlin, both in Oldsmobiles. Rounding out the top 10 finishers were: Alan Kulwicki, in a Ford (and the last driver to complete all 500 laps); Dale Jarrett, in a Ford; Earnhardt; Michael Waltrip, in a Pontiac and Ricky Rudd, in a Chevrolet.

Earnhardt ran a lap of 115.604 mph in winning the pole and Irvan averaged 91.782 mph in the race. Ten cautions slowed the race for 47 laps.

Irvan ran 178 Winston Cup races prior to his first win.

(Above) Dale Earnhardt (3) shoots by the wrecked Chevrolet of Ronnie Thomas after Thomas met the wall during the 1986 Valleydale 500.

(Far left) Kyle Petty is rewarded by Holston Distributing's Stuart Wood for setting the fastest time in second-round qualifying for the 1987 Valleydale Meats 500. He finished seventh in the race.

(Left) Morgan Shepherd returned to his roots when he competed in and won the 1987 Budweiser 200 Busch Series race. He finished eighth in the next day's Valleydale Meats 500.

(Below) Kyle Petty (21) "feels the heat" from "Daddy" during the '87 Valleydale Meats 500. Richard Petty finished second to race winner Dale Earnhardt.

(Left) Crew chief Harry Hyde and his driver, Tim Richmond, confer prior to the 1986 Busch 500. Characters in the 1990 movie, Days of Thunder, were based on the successful duo.

(Below) Dale Jarrett, in the No. 18 Eric Freedlander Chevrolet, sets up J.D. McDuffie's Pontiac for a pass in the '87 Valleydale Meats 500. Jarrett finished 10th, three laps down, while McDuffie exited early with a blown engine.

(Bottom right) Dale Earnhardt edges past Terry Labonte (11) during the Busch 500 on August 22, 1987. Labonte started on the pole and finished fourth.

(Bottom left) Richard and Judy Childress (from left) and Dale and Teresa Earnhardt enjoy victory lane after Earnhardt won the '87 Busch 500. The kid with the Wrangler hat in the rear? Looks like Dale Earnhardt Jr. to us!

Valleydale Meats 500
· · · · ·
April 14, 1991

*T*wo times during the race, Rusty Wallace was two laps down. He battled back, used a set of rules designed to enhance safety for crewmen working on cars during pit stops and beat Ernie Irvan to the win by one foot after starting on the pole.

The victory was all the more sweet because it was the first for his new team, of which he was a partial owner. Wallace drove a No. 2 Miller-sponsored (Roger) Penske Racing Pontiac and Irvan a No.4 Morgan-McClure Chevrolet.

"We hung it out, ran door to door and knocked each other on the last lap," Wallace said of the finish. "We had a whale of a race ... I just barely beat him."

Wallace definitely had an advantage on one restart because of an "odd-even" system instituted by NASCAR to ease congestion on pit road. Because Wallace was an "odd" numbered qualifier, he got to restart on the inside lane, which allowed him to shoot away from the field. The rule was in effect because of a pit-road accident at Atlanta the previous November.

Davey Allison finished third and Mark Martin fourth. Both drove Fords. Ricky Rudd rounded out the top five in a Chevrolet.

Wallace qualified at 118.051 mph and averaged 72.809 mph in the race. There were 19 cautions for 133 laps.

Bud 500
· · · · ·
August 24, 1991

*A*lan Kulwicki beat Sterling Marlin by about a straightaway to post his third career victory. Kulwicki, well off the pace at one point of the race, took the lead for keeps 137 laps later. He was driving his own Ford and Marlin was in a Junior Johnson-prepared Ford.

Actually, the driver of his own No. 7 Ford somehow got the better of a race track surface that tore up and crumbled throughout the 3-hour, 14-minute and 56-second race. The toll on tires was terrible and Kulwicki himself lost two laps in the pits early on because of tire problems. But he got back onto the lead lap on the 300th lap and took the lead for good 64 circuits later.

"I love to race on this track when it's right, but tonight it was breaking up," Kulwicki said. "We shouldn't have to come back and race on this surface. This track isn't up to par."

Ken Schrader finished third in a Hendrick Motorsports Chevrolet. Mark Martin was fourth in a Jack Roush Ford, followed by Ricky Rudd in a Hendrick Motorsports Chevrolet. Jimmy Spencer led from lap 113 through lap 317, but a throttle linkage problem and a penalty for bumping Martin dropped him from contention.

Bill Elliott won the pole at 116.957 mph. Kulwicki averaged 82.028 mph for the race. There were 11 cautions for 81 laps.

(Right) Bill Elliott had good reason to smile. The 1988 Valleydale Meats 500 was his first Winston Cup Series win on a short track.

(Far right , above and below) Dale Earnhardt had a reason to be happy, too. The day before Elliott's victory, Earnhardt drove his own No. 8 Goodwrench Chevrolet to victory in the Budweiser 200 Busch Series race.

(Below) Basketball star Brad Daugherty poses with Rusty Wallace after the driver was quickest in second-round qualifying for the 1988 Busch 500.

(Below right) Ernie Irvan waits while his U.S. Racing crew services his No. 2 Kroger Chevrolet during the 1988 Valleydale Meats 500.

(Top) In a NASCAR Winston Cup Series career that began in 1979 and lasted through 1994, Harry Gant spent much of it as the No. 33 "Skoal Bandit." Gant notched pole-position starts at Bristol in 1985, '87 and '94.

(Above) Rusty Wallace and his team owner, Raymond Beadle (right) had a good reason to be proud. Wallace survived a record 20 yellow flags to win the 1989 Valleydale Meats 500.

(Left) In 1989, Mark Martin was in his second season driving for Jack Roush. Through 2000, Martin won two races at Bristol and started on the pole six times.

Food City 500
· · · · ·
April 5, 1992

*A*lan Kulwicki fell in love with Bristol when he won his second straight race at the 0.533-mile track. Kulwicki, who had not won a Winston Cup event since the summer of 1991 at Bristol, edged Dale Jarrett for the victory after the two battled door-to-door the last 50 laps. Kulwicki was in his own No. 7 Hooters-sponsored Ford, and Jarrett was driving a No. 18 Interstate Batteries Chevrolet for a brand-new Joe Gibbs Racing team.

Kulwicki took the lead away from Jarrett on lap 474 and motored away to a narrow 0.72-second victory.

Ken Schrader finished third in a Hendrick Motorsports Chevrolet. Terry Labonte was fourth in the Billy Hagan Oldsmobile, and Dick Trickle rounded out the top five in the Stavola Brothers Ford. Both were one lap down.

As usual, there was plenty of action on the 36-degree-banked track that resulted in 10 caution flags for 75 laps. Crashes, however, sidelined just three of the 32 starters, while engine failure stopped just two more.

Rounding out the top 10 finishers were Ricky Rudd (Chevrolet), Morgan Shepherd (Ford), Hut Stricklin (Chevrolet), Rusty Wallace (Pontiac) and Derrike Cope (Chevrolet).

Kulwicki won the pole at 122.474 mph and averaged 86.316 mph for the race. For his run of 3 hours, 5 minutes and 15 seconds he picked up the top prize of $83,360.

Bud 500
· · · · ·
August 29, 1992

*T*rack president Larry Carrier knew he had a problem with his beloved race track. Because of its high banks and the pounding it took from 1,500-2,000 laps of competition each year, the asphalt surface just wasn't holding up.

So he decided on a radical solution. Carrier resurfaced his 0.533-mile bullring with concrete – something absolutely unheard of at the time. Teams tested prior to the summer race, and then when it came time for the showdown, Darrell Waltrip held the best hand. In his own DarWal Chevrolet, Waltrip led the final 133 laps and ran away with the race to post his 83rd career victory and his 12th at this high-banked oval. He easily outdistanced Dale Earnhardt, who finished second a distant 9.28 seconds behind the No. 17 Western Auto Chevrolet. Ken Schrader was third, in a Chevrolet, Kyle Petty finished fourth, in a Pontiac, and Alan Kulwicki was fifth in a Ford.

"Running on top of concrete sure beats the alternative – running into it," quipped Waltrip. "If they work on it and get it a little smoother, it will be a great place to race."

Eight drivers exchanged the lead 14 times. The caution waved 10 times for 55 laps. Ernie Irvan won the pole at 120.535 mph. Waltrip averaged 91.198 mph for the race and won $73,050.

(Right) Alan Kulwicki ran his first Winston Cup race in 1985 and captured his first of three poles at Bristol in 1988. He also won two races at the track and died in a plane crash en route to BMS on April 1, 1993.

(Below) Kulwicki (7) leads Rick Wilson (4) and Sterling Marlin during the 1989 Valleydale Meats 500. Kulwicki started third and finished 20th.

Food City 500
· · · · ·
April 4, 1993

*I*t was the most emotional weekend in the long history of Larry Carrier's speedway.

Defending NASCAR Winston Cup Series champion Alan Kulwicki lost his life in a private airplane accident en route to the track three days before the race. His twin-engine plane was arriving in Blountville, near, Bristol, about 10:30 p.m. after Kulwicki had made a public relations appearance in Knoxville for Hooters, his sponsor. Two other passengers and the pilot were also aboard the aircraft that crashed during its landing approach. There were no survivors.

After the Kulwicki team's 18-wheel car hauler made a ceremonial lap around the track and left, Rusty Wallace, in the No. 2 Penske Racing Pontiac, went on to win the race by a straightaway over Dale Earnhardt, driving the Richard Childress Chevrolet. Kyle Petty was third in a Pontiac, Jimmy Spencer fourth in a Ford, and Davey Allison, also in a Ford, was fifth.

Wallace was strong throughout the event and led it four times. He went to the front for the final time on lap 375 and was 0.82-second in front of Earnhardt at the finish. After he knew the race was his, he flipped his car around and made a clockwise "Polish victory lap" around the oval in honor of Kulwicki.

Wallace started from the pole, qualifying at 120.938 mph. He averaged 84.730 mph for the race.

Bud 500
· · · · ·
August 28, 1993

*M*ark Martin came from two laps down to blow by Rusty Wallace 13 laps from the finish, winning by 0.14-second. Martin was driving a Roush Racing Ford, and Wallace drove a Penske Racing South Pontiac. Dale Earnhardt was third in a Chevrolet, followed by Harry Gant in a Chevy and Rick Mast in a Ford.

Martin went into the lead for the final time 13 laps from the finish. Just three laps from the checkered flag, he not only had to think about the relentless Wallace but several slower cars in front of him. One of them was Geoff Bodine, who was trying to stay on the lead lap (which he did). While Martin had some less-than-kind things to say about Bodine, the driver of the No. 15 Ford said he didn't know he was in the way and wouldn't have deliberately tried to block Martin or Wallace.

Martin lost his laps after pitting early because of a vibration. By the halfway point, though, he was back on the lead lap and heading toward victory.

Martin won the pole at 121.405 mph and averaged 88.172 for the race. His win was worth $80,125.

The caution flag was out 11 times for 71 laps.

(Left and inset) Davey Allison's Winston Cup Series career began in the mid-1980s and was tragically cut short before he could try to match his famous father's record at Bristol. He did, however, win the 1990 Valleydale Meats 500.

(Below left) Dale Earnhardt didn't make too many mistakes at Bristol, but he lost it in the 1991 Valleydale Meats 500 and plowed into Sterling Marlin's No. 22 Maxwell House Ford. Marlin was through for the day while Earnhardt finished 20th.

(Below) Ernie Irvan's first Winston Cup career win came in the August 1990 Busch 500. It was also the first victory for his Virginia-based Morgan-McClure team.

(Above) It's considered by many to be one of the biggest engineering marvels in motor racing. Shortly after Alan Kulwicki won the April 1992 Food City 500, Larry Carrier assembled a construction crew, who tore up the track's asphalt surface and replaced it with concrete. The speedway was ready for that year's August Bud 500, which was won by Darrell Waltrip.

(Right) The hood goes up on Wally Dallenbach's Roush Racing Keystone Ford during the 1993 Bud 500. Dallenbach finished the race but was 64 laps down.

Food City 500
· · · · ·
April 10, 1994

*T*hree drivers ended up in the lead lap with Dale Earnhardt in front. The "Man in Black" took the lead from Geoff Bodine on lap 318 and led to the finish in his Richard Childress-owned Chevrolet.

Ken Schrader finished second in another Chevy, and Lake Speed was third in a Ford. Bodine finished fourth in a Ford, and Michael Waltrip, in a Pontiac, rounded out the top five.

Unfortunately for Bodine, the fortunes of racing went against him and, instead, favored Earnhardt. Bodine, in the No. 7 Exide Ford, took the lead on lap 170 and led until he made a green-flag pit stop for tires on lap 317. That put Earnhardt in the lead, and when the ninth of 10 caution flags was thrown six laps later, that allowed Earnhardt to pit and still keep the lead. It also played into the hands of Schrader and Speed, while Bodine went a lap down.

Rounding out the top 10 were Bobby Labonte, Rusty Wallace, Sterling Marlin, Bobby Hamilton and Dave Marcis.

Five drivers exchanged the lead 11 times, while seven were eliminated by accidents. Earnhardt averaged 89.647 mph and won by 7.63 seconds over Schrader. Chuck Bown started from pole position in a Ford. He qualified at 124.946 mph but ended up finishing 23rd.

Goody's 500
· · · · ·
August 27, 1994

*R*usty Wallace, sporting a new gold driving suit with black trim instead of the black outfit he'd worn the last couple of years, ended up edging Mark Martin by less than half a second to lead a one-two Ford finish. Dale Earnhardt was third and Darrell Waltrip fourth, both in Chevrolets. Bill Elliott rounded out the top five in a Ford.

Ten drivers swapped the lead 16 times in the action-packed event, but it was Wallace who took the lead from Geoff Bodine on lap 456 and led to the finish. Bodine, at first, looked like he was headed toward his third win of the season. But a broken water pump led to a blown engine, and Bodine dropped out on the 456th lap and finished 23rd.

Accidents took out nine of the 36 starters. The list of casualties included Dale Jarrett, Lake Speed, John Andretti, Bobby and Terry Labonte and Jeff Gordon.

Wallace averaged 91.363 mph, despite 12 cautions for 73 laps.

Harry Gant captured the pole position in a Chevrolet with a speed of 124.186 mph. He ran strong but "burned up" his tires late in the event and finished ninth, a lap down.

Food City 500
• • • • •
April 2, 1995

Goody's 500
• • • • •
August 26, 1995

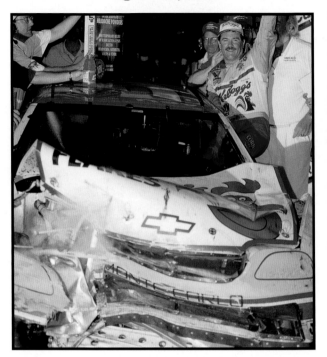

Jeff Gordon averaged 92.011 mph and soundly beat Rusty Wallace by 5.74 seconds after leading the last 98 laps. Gordon notched his third win of the year – and his first ever in the series on a short track – in the No. 24 Hendrick Motorsports/DuPont Chevrolet, while Wallace piloted the No. 27 Penske Racing South/Miller Genuine Draft Ford. Darrell Waltrip was third in a Chevrolet, Bobby Hamilton fourth in a Pontiac, and Ricky Rudd fifth in a Ford.

Dale Jarrett piloted the No. 28 Ford to a sixth-place finish and was the last driver to finish all 500 laps. The next three finishers, Terry Labonte, Mark Martin and Sterling Marlin, were a lap down and the 10th-place finisher, Robert Pressley, was two laps in arrears.

Gordon took the lead the final time on lap 402 from Mark Martin, who finished eighth, one lap down. Martin, in a Ford, won the pole with a speed of 124.605 mph.

Although there were seven caution flags for 65 laps, all but two of the 36 starters drove under the checkered flag. Greg Sacks dropped out on lap 213 with engine failure, and Kyle Petty, who qualified third quickest in the No. 42 Sabco Pontiac, crashed on lap 277.

Gordon completed the race in 2 hours, 53 minutes and 47 seconds, and five drivers exchanged the lead a dozen times.

Terry Labonte posted his third victory of the season the hard way. Second-place finisher Dale Earnhardt hit Labonte from behind as the two raced off the fourth turn on the final lap. Labonte's No. 5 Kellogg's machine hit the wall and skidded across the finish line first.

Under different circumstances, the "Iceman" might have melted. Instead, knowing what was about to happen, he gunned his engine and kept the car as straight as possible. Later, he just grinned and enjoyed himself in victory lane.

Both Labonte and Earnhardt were in Chevrolets. Dale Jarrett was third in a Ford, Darrell Waltrip fourth in a Chevy, and Mark Martin fifth in a Ford. Labonte took the lead from Jarrett on lap 432 and led to the finish.

Jeff Gordon, Sterling Marlin, Mike Wallace and Jeff Burton took finishing positions six through nine and were all on the lead lap. Derrike Cope, driving Bobby Allison's No. 12 Ford, was 10th, one lap down.

Labonte averaged 81.979 mph after 15 cautions slowed the race for 106 of its 500 laps. His take for the night was $66,940. Martin won the pole at 125.093 mph, while Labonte started second.

(Left) Strapped into the No. 4 Morgan-McClure/Kodak Film Chevrolet, Sterling Marlin is ready for the 1995 Food City 500.

(Below far left) Junie Donlavey has been a team owner almost as long as there's been a Winston Cup circuit. He was at the first Bristol race and is still active today.

(Below) Bobby Hamilton "drops in" for a chat prior to the '95 Food City 500. He drove the No. 43 STP Pontiac to a fourth-place finish.

(Upper left) Jeff Gordon started second in the '95 Food City 500 and won the race. He'd go on to win the championship that year.

(Left) By the time Larry Carrier relinquished ownership of Bristol International Raceway at the end of 1995, the track was truly thriving!

THE RACE FAN COMES FIRST

(Opposite page) Bruton Smith made stock car racing his passion and business many years ago. After looking at Bristol Motor Speedway, it took the founder of Speedway Motorsports, Inc. just minutes to decide to purchase it from Larry Carrier.

(Left) Smith wasted little time in starting to add his touch to the track. The construction of additional seating was one of his first projects.

The first time Olin Bruton Smith took a serious look at Bristol Motor Speedway, he waited only about 10 minutes before he made an offer to buy the place. His offer was accepted, give or take a few million, but quick business deals with sound reasoning is the trademark of racing's most successful entrepreneur.

"Well," he said in a very soft and gentlemanly tone, "I bought Bristol Motor Speedway for all the reasons you can see."

Just acquiring the "World's Fastest Half Mile-Track" did not fulfill Smith's dream. His creative mind was busy calculating all the next moves. So he started by tearing down a mountain and the sides of two other peaks. Without a grimace, he moved 2.5 million cubic yards of Tennessee rock and soil. He was on a mission and having as much fun as a kid in a new sandbox. You see, when Smith purchased the speedway from Larry Carrier in 1996,

the seating capacity was 71,000. Now the place holds 147,000 die-hard race fans, and soon the capacity will reach more than 165,000. Only about 28,000 of the original seats remain from when Smith bought the track. He has replaced the others with modern new grandstands. He has virtually torn down all the old grandstands except the ones along the backstretch, and those are soon to go.

"My goal is to make it a better place," Smith said. "And my plan is to continue making improvements. I understand when I first made the purchase that there were people who thought I was buying it only to move the (Winston Cup Series) race dates elsewhere. That was never my intention. I truly found something I was looking for at Bristol. I believe Bristol is phenomenal, much like Green Bay (Wis.), where everybody stands behind their Packers. It's like a Magic Kingdom, in both Virginia and Tennessee."

Ernie Irvan, in the No. 28 Texaco Havoline Ford, keeps the QVC Ford of Geoffrey Bodine at bay during the 1996 Food City 500. Close behind are Brett Bodine (11) Joe Nemechek (87), Robert Pressley (33) and Bobby Hamilton.

Smith's company, Speedway Motorsports Inc., also owns Atlanta Motor Speedway, in Hampton, Ga.; Las Vegas Motor Speedway; Lowe's Motor Speedway near Charlotte; the racing rights to Sears Point Raceway, in Sonoma, Calif., and Texas Motor Speedway near Fort Worth. He and Bob Bahre each purchased half of North Wilkesboro (N.C.) Speedway in 1996 and closed it at the end of the year. Bahre took one of the track's Winston Cup Series race dates and moved it to his speedway in Loudon, N.H. Smith took the other and had it transferred to his Texas track, which opened in 1997. .

State Street in Bristol is the state line. One side of the street is in Tennessee and the other side in Virginia. The "Volunteer State" may collect all the tax revenue derived from the speedway, but if Virginia chose to claim it, too, not too many people would really complain.

Smith smiled and added: "The difference in Bristol and Green Bay, however, is that we had more people on our waiting list for tickets than the Packers do. The place and its people are simply amazing. Every city, every country and every state in the United States could come here (Bristol) and take lessons. I mean that. There is no greater place to do business, or at least no greater place that I have ever found. People here treat me so nice that sometimes I pinch myself to make sure I am not dreaming. Everybody helps everybody here."

Smith has done his share of helping, too. With him, it's a give-and-take proposition with the area's residents.

"The difference in Bristol and Green Bay, however, is that we had more people on our waiting list for tickets than the Packers do. The place and its people are simply amazing..." — O. Bruton Smith

(Below left) Bill Elliott's "Drive Through Crew" changes an engine in the McDonald's Ford before the '96 Food City 500, which was shortened to 342 laps because of rain.

(Bottom left) Dale Earnhardt experienced a lot of success at Bristol, and provided a bit of controversy on more than one occasion.

(Bottom right) Larry McReynolds (left) and Ernie Irvan made a good crew chief-driver combination at Robert Yates Racing, although they didn't win together at Bristol.

(Below) Members of Dick Trickle's Healthsource team thank the fans for putting up with a rain delay during the '96 Food City 500.

Food City 500
· · · · ·
March 31, 1996

*A*s it turned out, the capacity crowd of fans at Bristol had a bit more time to do some shopping at the local Food City store after Jeff Gordon, driver of the No. 24 Hendrick Motorsports/DuPont Chevrolet had collected his second consecutive spring race victory at Bristol.

The reason was simple: After inclement weather had plagued the area all day, NASCAR officials finally were forced to end the event after 342 of its scheduled 500 laps were in the books.

The first Bristol race under the ownership of Bruton Smith's Speedway Motorsports, Inc., got the green flag 30 minutes late. Pole winner Mark Martin led the first 59 laps in his No. 6 Roush Racing Ford but after relinquishing the lead under caution would never head the field again. Bobby Labonte, Ricky Rudd, Rusty Wallace and Gordon swapped the lead until rain brought out the yellow flag on lap 321. After about a half hour, the race resumed, but a caution flag for a wreck and then more rain brought it to a premature conclusion.

Gordon's teammate, Terry Labonte, finished second, Martin was third, Dale Earnhardt fourth and Rusty Wallace fifth. Rounding out the top 10 were Dale Jarrett (Ford), Bobby Labonte (Chevrolet), Dick Trickle (Ford), Ricky Craven (Chevrolet) and Michael Waltrip (Ford).

Jarrett did a fine job in protecting his lead in Winston Cup points. He qualified seventh fastest, but on his second lap in time trials, he smacked the wall. He was forced into a backup car and had to start the race in the rear of the field.

Goody's Headache Powder 500
· · · · ·
August 24, 1996

*B*ruton Smith wasted little time in putting his mark on "Thunder Valley" since his company took possession of it earlier in the year. Now officially known as "Bristol Motor Speedway," there was already evidence of the new owner's plans for the track. Massive amounts of earth had been moved in preparation for new grandstands, and as a track spokesperson asked the fans to "pardon the dust," Mark Martin was busy trying to win his fourth consecutive pole position at Bristol.

The driver of the No. 6 Roush Racing Ford succeeded with a 15.368-second lap around the 0.533-mile oval. That translated into a speed of 124.857 mph.

Martin led the race's first nine laps before giving way to No. 2 starter Jeff Gordon. The defending Winston Cup Series champion kept the No. 24 Hendrick Motorsports Chevrolet in front through lap 99 before ceding the lead to No. 2 Rusty Wallace.

Wallace ended up leaving everyone else in the dust and captured his sixth Bristol win 0.630-second in front of Gordon. Martin finished third, Dale Jarrett, in a Ford, was fourth and Terry Labonte was fifth, in a Chevrolet. Rounding out the top 10 finishers were Michael Waltrip and Jimmy Spencer, in Fords, Ward Burton, in a Pontiac, Ricky Rudd, in a Ford, and Bobby Hamilton, in a Pontiac.

Five drivers swapped the lead eight times in the 2-hour, 55-minute and 12-second event, and there were eight caution-flag periods for a total of 67 laps.

(Left) Patience! Everyone waits out a red-flag period for a rain delay during the '96 Food City 500. Any holdup during a race is hard on all concerned.

(Below) Terry Labonte (left) has won two races at Bristol Motor Speedway in the 1990s, as well as one pole position. His younger brother, Bobby (right), however, has yet to experience much success on the demanding oval.

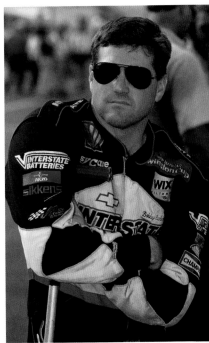

For instance, there's this story: One evening soon after he'd purchased the track a local civic organization hosted a dinner to raise money for area boys' and girls' clubs. That night $30,000 was collected. A bit later, Smith collared a group of community leaders and instructed them in the art of asking for money – and getting it. Then he told them if they raised $50,000 the following year he'd match it. With that incentive to spur them on, they did just that and Smith was as good as his word. Their next goal, Smith instructed, was $100,000. Raise it and he'd match it again. In 1999, the civic group goes after and gets $150,000 without batting an eye, and Smith matched that total. The two charities, Boys and Girls Club and Girls, Inc., raised $600,000 with Smith's help.

Smith, you see, has a soft spot for kids. He lost an infant son in 1984, and soon after he was instrumental in founding Speedway Children's Charities. The non-profit entity that specializes in raising funds that are given to groups that specialize in aiding children in need. It's head-quartered in Charlotte, with Thomas M. Sadler, a retired Air Force major general as its executive director. Every SMI track has its own chapter. Each, basically, does its own fund raising, but the money all goes in the same pot. Bristol Motor Speedway, for instance, gives away over $250,000 annually. The Bristol chapter is headed by Claudia Byrd.

The speedway and the Bristol area are virtually married to each other. Every Christmas, starting in 1997, the speedway hosts its "Fantasy In Lights," an incredible display that illuminates the area for miles that Byrd developed as a fund raiser.

(Below) In a career that started in 1993, Jeff Gordon's been able to put the No. 24 Hendrick Motorsports/DuPont Chevrolet into victory lane four times.

(Bottom) This multicar melee brought out one of the 12 caution flags for 97 laps in the 1997 Goody's Headache Powder 500.

"The speedway is a business with me, but the people in this town and this area treat me like family," Smith said.

Thousands of lights inside the oval track and drag strip are strung in such a manner that visitors can drive slowly through the entire facility and enjoy the spirit of Christmas. According to track officials, nearly a quarter-million people visit during the holidays. There's a small charge, but the money goes to children's-based charities.

Nonprofit organizations help with this and other projects, and in return the speedway aids these groups. More than 2,000 people help out during race weeks. Some are paid for their services, but most are volunteers from the various nonprofit groups. The money earned goes to their organizations.

"The speedway is a business with me, but the people in this town and this area treat me like family," Smith said.

At first glance Smith knew he wanted to make a lot of improvements. Aside from increasing the seating capacity, he wanted more restrooms. He knew he had to increase parking, and he said he needed another front door to the grounds.

"First come the race fans," he said, "and I think the fans will see that we've tried to think of everyone here with all the projects we have completed. First come the race fans. Always. Everything we do is to make this a more fan-friendly facility. We also try to make things better for the drivers and the team owners, as well."

Smith has not turned a shovel full of dirt out of fear. "Listen," he said, "Bristol could have gone on for years just as it was, without any improvements. In racing, however, there comes a point where you have to get more involved or you have to get out. To get more involved means spending more money all the time to upgrade your facility. There is no turning back now. All race tracks have to continue improving their facilities or they will just go away. It takes a lot of money to operate a race track, but I think all tracks are making money."

Smith believes NASCAR is no better than its facilities and noted that "this is the way it should be." Keeping that in mind, he also talked of further plans for the facility. Replacing the last remaining vestage of the original track, the concrete backstretch grandstands, is on his project list for the near future. He and his closest advisers have also considered running both NASCAR Winston Cup Series races at night, but right now that's just an idea. Soon after the purchase of the speedway, Smith began acquiring more acreage to help handle the parking. He bought a bit of land here and a bit more there until he increased the grounds by 581 acres. He cropped off a mountain and that

"At Bristol first come the race fans. Always. Everything we do is to make this a more fan-friendly facility," — O. Bruton Smith

(Top left) Jeremy Mayfield (37) and Lake Speed battle it out during the 1997 Goody's Headache Powder 500. They finished 30th and 29th, respectively.

(Bottom left) Derrike Cope "skittled" into one of the several accidents during the '97 Goody's 500, but he got through it and went on to finish 32nd.

(Below) Mark Martin leads a long pack out of turn four during the '97 Goody's 500. Martin lost the lead to eventual winner Dale Jarrett on lap 469 and finished second.

added more than 2,000 new parking spaces, but Smith knows he needs more.

What Smith has done to the track is really no more than a reflection of the man himself. Citing his love for "building things," he has constructed a business empire that focuses on the racing and automotive industries. Profiled in the 1996 edition of Forbes magazine's "Forbes 400," Smith was listed as the 187th richest person in America. He was again featured in Forbes' 1997 and '98 editions.

(Top) Like most tracks, Bristol has set aside a restricted "camping" area for the competitors and their families, where they can relax and socialize.

(Above) Bruton Smith (right) recognized all-time Bristol winner Darrell Waltrip in April 1997 by naming a grandstand in his honor.

(Top right) Sterling Marlin (4) slips underneath Lance Hooper during the '97 Goody's Headache Powder 500.

(Above right) There were no "close calls" for Brett Bodine in the '97 Goody's 500 – or Ricky Rudd, in the No. 10 Tide Ford, for that matter!

Smith is a native "Tarheel." He grew up on a farm in rural Stanly County, N.C., near Oakboro and got involved in auto race promotion back in the 1950s when NASCAR itself was just a fledgling organization. In organized stock car racing's early years, Smith was one of the first "professional" promoters who paid drivers decent purses, tended to the needs of the fans and found unique ways to promote events staged at speedways he leased in North Carolina.

Smith's first big-time venture in the sport came when he teamed up with legendary driver (and flashy business entrepreneur) Curtis Morton Turner in the late '50s. After noting the success of both Darlington (S.C.) Raceway and Daytona International Speedway, Smith and Turner figured the future of the sport would be found in super-speedway racing. Each wanted to build a big track near Charlotte, N.C. Both knew, however, two tracks in the same vicinity wouldn't work. So they went in together and sold stock in the venture. Charlotte Motor Speedway (now

Lowe's Motor Speedway) opened in June 1960 with the longest NASCAR race on the circuit – the World 600. While the speedway drew crowds, it was undercapitalized and went into bankruptcy. It later became the first North Carolina corporation to survive reorganization under Chapter 11 requirements.

During the track's reorganization, Smith left North Carolina to pursue other interests in Illinois and Texas, and working with Ford Motor Co., he opened several auto dealerships. At the same time, he began purchasing shares of stock in the Charlotte track, and by 1975 he'd become its major stockholder, regaining control of day-to-day operations. Since that time, he made millions of dollars of improvements to the facility, including thousands of new grandstand seats, condominiums, VIP suites, a "speedway club" and, in 1992, a $1.7 million lighting system that made the track the first superspeedway to be fully illuminated for nighttime events.

Food City 500
· · · · ·
April 13, 1997

*A*nother good day for Jeff Gordon spelled heartbreak for Rusty Wallace at Bristol.

Gordon, in a Chevrolet, passed Ford-driving Wallace on the final lap and won by less than a half-second. It was his third victory of a season that would see him go on to clinch his second NASCAR Winston Cup Series championship.

Battling it out in front of a crowd of 118,000 enthusiastic race fans, Gordon and Wallace soon established themselves as the leading contenders for victory. Between them they led 365 of the 500 laps, thus adding to the drama of the event.

Terry Labonte, Gordon's teammate, finished third in a Chevrolet. Dale Jarrett was fourth in a Ford, followed by Mark Martin in another Ford. Finishing sixth through 10th were Dale Earnhardt (Chevrolet), Bill Elliott (Ford), Chad Little (Pontiac), Jeremy Mayfield (Ford) and Brett Bodine (Ford).

Six drivers exchanged the lead 13 times. Gordon led laps 163 through 226, and laps 355 through 414. Wallace took over on lap 415 and led until the final lap.

Twenty cautions slowed the race for 132 laps. Gordon averaged 75.035 mph, while Wallace won the pole at 123.586 mph and led the first 49 laps.

Goody's 500
· · · · ·
August 23, 1997

*D*ale Jarrett led the final 30 laps and beat Mark Martin to the checkered flag by less than one second in another squeaker of a race at Bristol Motor Speedway.

The race, which marked 20 years of night racing at BMS, was filled with the "unexpectedly expected." Jeff Gordon, who started second in the No. 24 DuPont Refinishes Chevrolet, dominated the event's first half and appeared to be ready to win for the ninth time in 1997. The situation changed in a hurry, though, when Gordon and Jeremy Mayfield crashed on the backstraight, sending Gordon into the wall.

Gordon went behind the wall, lost more then 50 laps while his car was repaired, and he ended up finishing 35th, 135 laps behind.

This, in effect, opened the door for Jarrett's first win at Bristol, and more significantly, his initial Winston Cup victory on a short track.

Dick Trickle was third and Jeff Burton fourth. The top four drove Fords, while Steve Grissom was fifth in a Chevrolet. Jarrett averaged 80.013 mph after the caution waved 12 times for 97 laps. Five drivers exchanged the lead 12 times and Kenny Wallace won the pole in the No. 81 Square D Ford at 123.039 mph but was involved in an accident and finished 39th.

Forty-two cars started the 500-lap event and all but eight ran to the finish. Darrell Waltrip, the track's most successful driver, crashed on lap 116 and finished dead last.

In 1990, Smith purchased Atlanta International Raceway, changed the name to Atlanta Motor Speedway, and used the same "Charlotte" formula to completely revamp the facility. Five years later, he consolidated his motorsports holdings and formed Speedway Motorsports, Inc. The first motorsports company to ever be traded on the New York Stock Exchange, in addition to its six race tracks, SMI also provides, event, food, beverage and souvenir merchandising services through its Finish Line Events subsidiary and manufactures several types of small-scale race cars through another subsidiary, 600 Racing. Smith's retail auto group was organized under the Sonic Automotive banner in 1997 and owns and operates more then 150 cars dealerships nationwide. Through Sonic Financial Corp., Smith also has several other business holdings in insurance and real estate.

Smith did not just walk in and kick the door open when he purchased the track he eventually renamed Bristol Motor Speedway. He very carefully hand picked his leaders, including Jeff Byrd, BMS' vice president and general manager.

Byrd, a Winston-Salem native, was working in special events at R.J. Reynolds when Smith made him an offer he could not refuse. Smith had conferred with the late Ralph Seagraves, whom was once Byrd's boss. In fact, it was Seagraves, whose "down-home," "good ol' boy" persona hid a knack for business, promotion and just getting things done, who had hired Byrd in 1973. Seagraves was simply a highly effective public relations professional. Even after he retired in 1985, he remained "on the job" as a consultant for Reynolds almost until his death in September 1998.

A packed house was on hand to watch pole winner Rusty Wallace and No. 2 qualifier Jeff Gordon lead off the 1998 Food City 500. Gordon went on to win the race, while Wallace finished a disappointing 33rd.

Smith did not just walk in and kick the door open when he purchased the track he renamed Bristol Motor Speedway. He very carefully hand picked his leaders, including Jeff Byrd, BMS' vice president and general manager.

(Above left) Dale Earnhardt (3) pressures Mark Martin during the 1998 Food City 500. With a 37th-place start and 22nd-place finish, it was not a good day for the "Intimidator."

(Left) Terry Labonte held off the DuPont Chevrolet of teammate Jeff Gordon, in the '98 Food City 500, until Gordon got by on lap 439 and went on to win. Labonte and the "rooster" finished second, while pole winner Rusty Wallace brought the Miller Lite Ford home a disappointing 33rd.

(Below) Martin led no laps in the March 29 Food City event and finished seventh, on the lead lap.

"I knew the type person I wanted overseeing the speedway," Smith said, "and after talking with Seagraves and others, I knew Jeff was the person."

Hiring the right people along the way, buying additional acreage here and there, making vast improvements, and moving mountains takes time. But these are projects in the aftermath of a quick-draw business deal, and nobody puts a package together quicker or better than Bruton Smith. The man's insight at Bristol Motor Speedway, his creative ability to move mountains and make changes for the better, and his close bonding with the community are truly marvels in today's business world. ■

(Top) Digging up the concrete? No, just the opposite! Tons and tons of earth were laid down on Bristol's surface in preparation for a two-day World of Outlaws Sprint Car event in June 2000. The open-wheel "dirt daubers" put on a whale of a show before a large crowd.

(Above) More dirt? Well, lots of it was moved in 1997 while new grandstand construction was under way.

(Above right) Ernie Irvan runs hard to stay ahead of Steve Park's Pennzoil Chevrolet and the Budweiser Chevrolet of Wally Dallenbach in the 1998 Goody's Headache Powder 500.

(Right) Dale Earnhardt, here leading Kenny Wallace (81) and Bobby Hamilton, tried hard to win the '98 Goody's Headache Powder 500 but manage only a sixth-place finish.

Food City 500
· · · · ·
March 29, 1998

*T*his one was racing's version of All In the Family - or maybe better yet, Family Feud. Jeff Gordon and Terry Labonte, Chevrolet teammates at Hendrick Motorsports, had the crowd on its feet as they battled to the wire and finished one-two ahead of Dale Jarrett in a Ford. Jeff Burton and Johnny Benson, also in Fords, were fourth and fifth, respectively.

The outcome of this race was basically determined when its 12th caution period, brought out on lap 437 after Rusty Wallace crashed his No. 2 Penske Racing South Ford, saw Gordon, Labonte and Jarrett come into the pits. Gordon's pit was in front of Labonte's and Jarrett's stall was behind him. During the stop, Labonte kept his eye on Jarrett when it should have been on Gordon.

Gordon, in the No. 24 DuPont Chevrolet, shot back onto the track first and kept the lead the rest of the way. The victory tied him with Darrell Waltrip for the most consecutive victories in the spring race at Bristol.

Gordon beat Labonte by half a second. He averaged 82.850 mph, and 14 cautions slowed the race for 88 laps. Jarrett led laps 345 through 362. Labonte took over and led 363 through 437, and then Gordon grabbed the lead and led from 438 through 500. Ten drivers exchanged the lead 19 times.

Wallace won the pole with a speed of 124.275 mph. Gordon started on the outside front row.

Goody's Headache Powder 500
· · · · ·
August 22, 1998

*M*ark Martin (above) beat Roush Racing teammate Jeff Burton by more than two seconds to lead a Ford parade across the finish line. Martin, Burton, Rusty Wallace and Dale Jarrett were 1-2-3-4 in Fords, followed by Jeff Gordon in a Chevrolet.

In a way, Martin's victory came about seven days too late. He'd wanted to win the week before in Michigan, so he could dedicate the victory to his late father, Julian Martin, who had been so instrumental in starting his son's racing career. On Aug. 8, the elder Martin and his wife and stepdaughter all perished in a private plane crash.

"This (victory) was for them. They would have been proud of me tonight," Martin said in victory lane.

Martin started fourth, took the lead for the first time on lap 191 and held it for just nine laps. When he took it again on lap 320, however, it was his for keeps. At the checkered flag, he was a healthy 2.185 seconds in front of Burton.

Dale Earnhardt, who was sixth, led laps 278 through 311, and then Bobby Labonte took over from lap 312 through 319. Martin averaged 86.949 mph in the 3-hour, 3-minute and 54-second race and won $80,315 in notching his fifth victory of the season.

Wallace won the pole with a speed of 125.554 mph around the 0.533-mile track. Thirteen caution flags slowed the race for 86 laps.

A casual airborne observer flying over the speedway at night just might mistake it for a sports stadium in a densely packed urban area and might find it hard to believe something this impressive could be found in a semi-rural location!

(Left) Brett Bodine (11), Bobby Hamilton (4) and Dale Jarrett run "in formation" during the 1999 Food City 500.

(Below) Miss Winston and Rusty Wallace are on the receiving end of a champagne shower after Wallace won the '99 Food City 500.

(Middle left) Kyle Petty (44) feels some pressure from Steve Park during the '99 Food City 500.

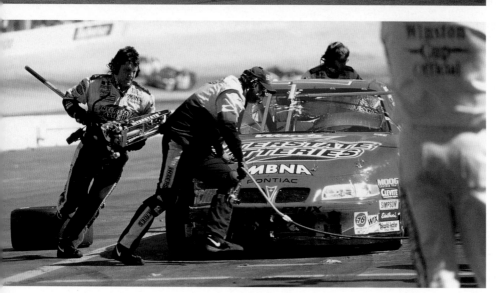

(Above) Bobby Labonte's "Battery Boys" get right to work during the '99 Food City event. It was a rough day for Labonte, who finished 37th.

(Right) Hail to the champ! The 1999 Goody's Headache Powder 500 would be Dale Earnhardt's final visit to Bristol's victory lane.

Food City 500
• • • • •
April 11, 1999

*R*usty Wallace started on the pole, led four times for 425 laps and on lap 352 he slipped by Mark Martin and led to the checkered flag, winning by 0.223-second over Martin.

The margin of victory meant that Martin's No. 6 Roush Racing Ford was right on the tail of Wallace's No. 2 Penske Racing South Ford at the finish. It was close!

"Mark Martin ... that's the guy I'm thinking about," Wallace said. "At the end he was really mowing me down. He got there and I held him off."

The win was Wallace's first of the season and 49th of his career. It was also the seventh time he'd gone into Bristol's victory circle.

Dale Jarrett finished third, also in a Ford. John Andretti was fourth, in a Pontiac, and Jeff Burton fifth, in a Ford. Sixth went to Jeff Gordon, Ted Musgrave was seventh, Kyle Petty, eighth, Ward Burton, ninth, and Dale Earnhardt, 10th.

Seven caution flags slowed the race for 57 laps. Wallace averaged 93.078 mph after winning the pole with a speed of 125.142 mph.

The lead changed hands only seven times among five drivers.

Goody's Headache Powder 500
• • • • •
August 28, 1999

*T*his slam-bang slugfest turned into the most controversial finish in the almost four-decade history of the speedway.

In this race, Terry Labonte slipped under Dale Earnhardt on the last lap coming off the second turn. Earnhardt then tagged the rear of Labonte's No. 5 Chevrolet, sending it into the wall. While thousands of fans filled the "bowl" with boos, Earnhardt drove his No. 3 black GM Goodwrench Chevrolet into victory lane. Labonte, his dreams of another victory quashed (and squashed!), finished eighth, one lap down.

The incident was an almost carbon copy of one at the track that involved the same two drivers four years ago. In that case, though, Labonte kept control of his spinning car and won.

After deliberating for about an hour, NASCAR officials announced that the victory would stand. The incident was purely a racing accident.

Jimmy Spencer finished second in a Ford, Ricky Rudd was third in a Ford, Jeff Gordon fourth in a Chevy and Tony Stewart was fifth in a Pontiac.

Earnhardt averaged 91.276 mph and finished the race in 2 hours, 55 minutes and 11 seconds. Ten times the caution waved for 60 laps. Tony Stewart started from the pole after qualifying at 124.589 mph.

(Right). Ward Burton, had his Caterpillar Pontiac at the front of the 2000 Food City 500 twice for 14 laps. It was a good day for the Virginia driver, who finished third.

(Below right) It was definitely not a good day for John Andretti (43), Dave Blaney (93) and Rick Mast in the 2000 version of the spring race. They crashed on lap 463 and brought out the last of 11 caution-flag periods.

(Top) Ricky Rudd gets "wired up" before the start of the 2001 Food City 500. Rudd started 14th and finished 10th, in the No. 28 Robert Yates Racing Ford. It was the Virginia driver's fourth top-10 finish of the still-young season.

(Left) Pit action was, to say the least, "lively" during the 2001 Food City 500. The crews of (from bottom to top) Jimmy Spencer, Matt Kenseth and Terry Labonte hustled to complete their jobs as quickly as possible. Of the three, only Labonte has won at Bristol.

(Below) One guy who certainly appears to have the Tennessee oval figured out is Rusty Wallace. The 1989 Winston Cup Series champion has nine victories at Bristol Motor Speedway.

(Above) Why does Bristol Motor Speedway attract sold-out crowds race after race? One good reason has to be the tight action produced on the track's high banks. There's no time to relax – for fans or drivers – as the excitement seems never to end!

(Right) Sterling Marlin, in the No. 40 Chip Ganassi-owned Dodge, was a strong presence during much of the latest Food City 500, but he faded at the end. Marlin started second, led five times for 81 laps and finished 12th.

Food City 500

$\bullet \bullet \bullet \bullet \bullet$

March 26, 2000

*R*usty Wallace fully took advantage of a little bit of charity on the part of teammate Jeremy Mayfield and the misfortunes of Dale Earnhardt and Jeff Gordon at Thunder Valley. The result was something the driver of the No. 3 Penske Racing South Ford had been yearning for – his 50th career NASCAR Winston Cup Series victory.

Most fittingly, the "Big 5-0" came at the same track – and in the same event – where he scored his first series win in 1986.

Early in the race, it appeared that either Chevrolet drivers Jeff Gordon or Dale Earnhardt would be headed into victory lane. Earnhardt started 11th and quickly charged toward the front of the field. Gordon, who started third, took the lead on lap 52, and except for one lap, he led the next 153 circuits. Earnhardt then grabbed the lead from Gordon on lap 206 but two laps later got caught up in a crash and had to go behind the wall for repairs.

From that point, the race was basically a three-way duel among Gordon, Mayfield and Wallace. At one point, Mayfield even let Wallace slip by to lead a lap for the five bonus points. Wallace led the final 75 laps and finished 1.622 seconds in front of the Pontiac of Johnny Benson. Ward Burton, Mayfield and Terry Labonte rounded out the top five, while Gordon finished eighth after losing time in the pits when his car hit a loose tire from another car.

GoRacing.com 500

$\bullet \bullet \bullet \bullet \bullet$

August 26, 2000

*R*usty Wallace again showed the world that he hadn't forgotten his short-track roots by starting on the pole and winning his ninth career Winston Cup series race at the 0.533-mile east Tennessee oval. The victory also meant that he'd made a "clean sweep" at Bristol in the final year of the 20th century.

This one, however, wasn't easy for the driver of the No. 2 Miller Lite Ford. With less than 50 laps left, Wallace had to avoid what he called a "huge wreck" in the first turn, and with just 11 laps to go, he almost plowed into a lapped car that had moved down in front of him. Still he was able to avoid calamity in a race that saw the yellow flag wave 13 times for 85 laps and finish 0.501-second in front of Tony Stewart's Pontiac. Mark Martin was third in a Ford, Dale Earnhardt finished fourth in a Chevrolet and Steve Park was fifth, also in a Chevrolet.

The race took 3 hours, 7 minutes and 15 seconds to complete. Wallace's share of the purse was $107,540.

(Above) Kevin Harvick – with Sterling Marlin in tow – passes by a memorial to the driver he replaced, during the 2001 Food City 500. Dale Earnhardt, a nine-time winner at Bristol, died in a racing accident in February at Daytona Beach, Fla. His No. 3 Chevrolet was renumbered 29 by the RCR Enterprises team and Harvick was given the ride.

(Below) Matt Kenseth (17) challenges Dale Jarrett during the '01 Food City event. They finished 14th and 16th, respectively, on the lead lap.

(Above) En route to victory: Elliott Sadler leads – in order – John Andretti, Tony Stewart, Jeremy Mayfield and Ward Burton in the Food City 500. Soon after this photo was taken, Sadler crossed the start-finish line first to record his initial Winston Cup Series victory.

Food City 500

· · · ·

March 25, 2001

It took Elliott Sadler 76 attempts – all but two of them with the Wood Brothers Racing team of Stuart, Va. – but patience finally paid off for both the team and its 25-year-old driver.

The Emporia, Va., native, driving the No. 21 Motorcraft Ford, took the lead for the final time on lap 431. He survived a bumping incident with Kevin Harvick (No. 29, below) 53 laps from the finish and captured his first NASCAR Winston Cup Series victory.

Sadler's win was a close one. He was just 0.426-second in front of the No. 43 Petty Enterprises Dodge of John Andretti (right) at the finish. Jeremy Mayfield finished third, in a Ford, Jeff Gordon was

fourth, in a Chevrolet, and Ward Burton was fifth, in a Dodge. Terry Labonte, Rusty Wallace, Bobby Hamilton, Steve Park and Ricky Rudd filled in the top 10.

Sadler's win was the 97th for the Woods team which had been competing since 1953. It was, however, the first short-track win for the team since February 1986 at Richmond, Va., and its first points-race victory of any sort since 1993 at Atlanta.

Sadler completed the event in 3 hours, 3 minutes and 54 seconds at an average speed of 86.949 mph and won $124,700. Mark Martin qualified at 126.303 mph to start on the pole.

racin' the way it ought'a be!

(Opposite page above) It takes a crew to race a car and a team to operate a track. The Bristol Motor Speedway team includes, from left to right: Harmon Simcox; Bob King; Dede Hash; Logan McCabe; Evelyn Hicks; Fred King; Darlene Carrier; Wayne Estes and Jeff Byrd.

(Opposite page below) What would you get if you covered Bristol Motor Speedway's racing surface with 1,500 truckloads of clay? You'd have a track that hosts two weekends of dirt races each June — with 100,000 more seats than any other track in the world.

(Left) Jeff Byrd (right) and his wife, Claudia (left) have enjoyed meeting and mixing with racing's elite over the years. Among those with the couple at this banquet in the 1980s are two of Bristol's owners, Larry Carrier (next to Byrd) and Warner Hodgdon (fourth from right).

Along the way there were several critical junctures in the history of Bristol Motor Speedway. Of course, Larry Carrier's and Carl Moore's original decision to bring stock car racing to the hills of east Tennessee may seem to be the most important aspect of the track, but there were many other factors that went into Bristol becoming NASCAR's most popular venue.

This evolution wouldn't have happened without the decisions that made Bristol Motor Speedway different from other NASCAR-sanctioned tracks. Together, the changes have combined to make Bristol the "toughest ticket in racing." Would the same cult-like following have developed without the radical decisions?

It's possible but not probable.

Perhaps the track was just predestined to become what it is today. A Mecca of racing that all true fans ultimately have to experience for their lives to be complete.

Who knows what made Carrier decide to change the banking to 36 degrees – the steepest of any track in the sport. What inspired Gary Baker to light the speedway for night racing? And Carrier's move to concrete the track may have been made of necessity, but it was just one other thing that makes Bristol different from the rest.

Bruton Smith's vision took the track and its reputation (as well as its grandstands!) to new heights. No one could have pictured a half-mile bullring with 147,000 seats and 100 skyboxes – no one except Smith. Part of the magic of Bristol is simply this: After Smith's rebuilding program, the facility is almost brand-new. The racing itself, however, is still the old-fashioned beating and banging that reminds fans of what the sport used to be. In fact, the most famous quote about the place came from a Winston Cup driver, who said when asked how it feels to race at Bristol, "It's like flying a F-16 in a high school gym."

(Top) Bristol Motor Speedway is truly a "21st century" facility. It offers the race fan all the comforts one might expect a modern sports stadium to provide – plus a night-time NASCAR Winston Cup Series race that's rarely anything but exciting. The Bristol experience really is "racin' the way it oughta be!"

(Above) Bristol Motor Speedway's Director of Operations Scott Hatcher (right), here with operations supervisor Rick Kerns, has been instrumental in the growth and expansion of the track since it was purchased by Bruton Smith in 1996.

In the end, it's a combination of unrelated factors tied together by the people who love the track like it was a part of their respective families that makes Bristol special.

There are fans who have given up tickets to other events so they can make those two trips a year to "The World's Fastest Half Mile." Many have come for each of the speedway's 40 years of existence, but their eyes still light up when they turn onto Volunteer Parkway, and see the hulking steel-and-aluminum structure come into view. It has become a never-ending love story with new chapters written each spring and fall.

There is also the story of the folks who make a living working at Bristol Motor Speedway. These are the individuals who truly believe that the future of the race track depends on them and the care and devotion they have for the track. The speedway began as a family project of the Carriers and Moores and continued in that mode for years. Even today, after growing to become

one of the country's largest spectator facilities, the family aspect of the speedway remains strong for the people who work there.

When Smith purchased the speedway in 1996, he searched the sport for someone to lead it. Smith consulted with Ralph Seagraves, a retired R.J. Reynolds Tobacco Co. sports marketing executive, who suggested that Smith offer Jeff Byrd the job. Byrd, the vice president of business development for Reynolds' Sports Marketing Enterprises, had worked in the motorsports industry for more than two decades and was quite familiar with the business aspects of racing.

"I talked with Bruton several times and he was very persuasive," Byrd said. "Still, it was going to be very tough for me to leave my company of 23 years and move my family out of Winston-Salem, N.C. (his hometown)."

Smith eventually prevailed, like he always seems to do, and Byrd was headed to Bristol Motor Speedway as its vice president and general manager. He thought he was in for a life of marketing and public relations while making an occasional speech to a civic group. Little did he know that he would spend the next four years of his life dressed in jeans and boots while getting a graduate-level education in the construction business.

"The first time Bruton showed up in Bristol, we got in my truck and he took me on a tour," Byrd recalled. "He started talking about moving mountains and building grandstands and tearing down perfectly good buildings. At that point in time, I wondered what I was in for.

"Not only did he tell me the exact progression of the different construction projects, he told me how much he expected the track to make in each succeeding year. Looking back, the construction occurred just like he envisioned it, and it's truly amazing how close he was to the profitability of the speedway."

When Byrd arrived at the track, Byrd found a group of employees who were just as unsure about its future as he'd been. However, they hadn't heard the "gospel according to Bruton" and had no idea what lay in front of them personally.

"I quickly found out that Larry Carrier had surrounded himself with really talented and dedicated people," Byrd said. "In people like Harmon Simcox; Bob King; DeDe Hash; Evelyn Hicks; Darlene Carrier; Fern Greenway and Sonya Moore, he had put together a team that allowed the speedway to operate smoothly while giving Larry time to enjoy his other pursuits, his family and his boxing business."

In the end, it's a combination of unrelated factors tied together by the people who love the track like it was a part of their respective families that makes Bristol special.

In time, Byrd discovered that the two NASCAR Winston Cup races were not enough to keeps his talented staff occupied. Adding seasoned professionals like Fred King (vice president of finance), Scott Hatcher (present operations director) Logan McCabe (marketing and sales director), Wayne Estes (communications director) and Ben Trout (manager of public relations) to the team served as a catalyst for new ideas and events.

As construction progressed the watchful eye of Smith and his team of engineers, the schedule at Bristol Motor Speedway began to expand as quickly as the new grandstands.

"It seemed like a shame to have such a wonderful facility that people loved to visit and only use it two weekends a year," noted Byrd. "We had assembled one of the most creative and energetic teams in sports, and they wanted to do more."

One of the first new events was the brainchild of Byrd's wife, Claudia. Smith had charged her with the responsibility of organizing and funding the Bristol chapter of Speedway Children's Charities.

"I wanted to do something different to raise money. This area already had several traditional fund-raisers such as galas or golf tournaments," she said. "I also wanted to start something that the children themselves could enjoy while at the same time raising money for non-profit organizations."

Claudia Byrd adroitly melded the two ideas, and the result was the "Fantasy in Lights" holiday spectacular, a three-mile drive around the speedway and dragway grounds that features more than 1.5 million lights and over 70 customized displays. More than a million people have since visited what has by now become a Christmas tradition in the Tri-Cities region. Volunteer groups staff the event, and the resulting profits have benefited thousands of children. Chief electrician Larry Stike has become the keeper of the lights, and he prides himself on developing new and exciting attractions each holiday season.

After two winters of adding to the seat count at the oval track, Smith reasoned that a world-class speedway shouldn't be the neighbor of a drag strip of distinctly lesser quality. So he brought out the dynamite and bulldozers

(Above left) Old seating had to be torn out so it could be replaced with new and expanded accommodations. By 2002, the track will be able to hold 165,000 people.

(Top and above) The new owners plans for the track included moving earth – tons of it! Today, the speedway little resembles what was put in place in 1961.

More than a million people come to Bristol Motor Speedway annually to see its "Fantasy In Lights" Christmas season spectacular, a three-and-a-half-mile drive around the track and through the drag strip. There are more than a million and a half holiday lights.

once again and set about reconstructing the fabled Thunder Valley Dragway. A million yards of rock and dirt later, Thunder Valley reassumed its role as one of the premier drag racing facilities in the world. After two years of hosting drag racing's all-star event, Bristol rejoined the national event schedule of the National Hot Rod Association (NHRA) with the running of the MAC Tools Thunder Valley Nationals.

During this time period Byrd and his colleagues spent countless hours trying to put down on paper just what made Bristol so special. They knew what the elements were but couldn't come up with an explanation that sounded right. Then a telephone call came that put everything into perspective. It was the solution Byrd and company had been trying to find.

"I love answering the phone and talking to fans who call the speedway," Byrd said. "Unfortunately, many of them are looking for tickets, and we hate to disappoint them."

One such fan called to inquire about tickets. He told Byrd he'd seen the Bristol night race on ESPN and just had to have tickets to next year's event.

"He said he was tired of going to all those tracks where nothing ever happened," Byrd recalled. "He said he wanted to come to Bristol Motor Speedway because it was the only place left where 'NASCAR has racin' the way it oughta be.'"

Byrd couldn't wait to tell the promotions department what the fan had said. Everyone at Bristol agreed that "Racin' The Way It Oughta Be" described the track perfectly.

Nothing, however, could describe the reception Byrd and Estes got at company headquarters when, in late 1999, they told Smith and Speedway Motorsports President H.A. "Humpy" Wheeler their latest idea for a new event. Estes had come up with an unbelievable scenario: Cover the 0.533-mile concrete, high-banked oval with red clay and stage dirt-track races for two weeks in June.

"Bruton and Humpy thought we had gone crazy," Byrd admitted. "They said it would be impossible to put the dirt on and even harder to get it off in time for the August Winston Cup weekend."

Byrd and Estes prevailed, though, and supervised by Scott Hatcher of BMS, the dirt went down and the people showed up. More than 100,000 dirt-track fans got a taste of what NASCAR race followers had known all along – Bristol is different! The United Dirt Track Racing Association (UDTRA) Late Models and the winged Sprint Cars of the World of Outlaws (WoO) raced in front of record crowds and established a new June "tradition" at Bristol.

Symphony and country music concerts now share time on the Bristol calendar along with Monster Truck, auto fairs and tractor pulls. Boy Scouts of America expositions and cancer research fundraisers are much-anticipated events that appeal to local residents, and various driving schools set up shop at Bristol several times each year

In 2000, more than a million people attended events at Bristol!

Through it all, one constant remains. That's the desire to remember who made the speedway special to begin with – the people.

It's the people who come 147,000 strong for the Busch Series and Winston Cup circuit weekends ... the grandparents who bring the youngsters to "Fantasy in Lights" every Christmas ... the employees who clock in each day with the continuing mission to keep Bristol Motor Speedway No. 1 in customer satisfaction.

"It's really simple when you think about it," Byrd said. "The track gives the fans what they want in terms of drama and action, and we just treat them the way we would want to be treated if we came to an event at Bristol. We've been really blessed, and we try to give the fans something back everyday." ■

The Toughest Ticket In Motorsports

There was an old man back in the hills of Tennessee ... way back in the hills ... so far back in the hills, in fact, that he used owls for house cats and cougars for lap dogs.

Other than some hunting, fishing and trapping, all he did was pan the creeks for gold. One day the old man came to town, and a banker met him on the street. The banker, realizing his own value if the old gentleman struck it rich, asked if he had ever found any gold in those creeks. "No, none at all," the old man said, "but I am incredibly persistent."

"Where, may I ask," the banker inquired, "did you learn to use such fluent language?"

"From my son," the old man replied. "For several years now he's been saying you have to be incredibly persistent to get a ticket to one of them NASCAR races down yonder at Bristol Motor Speedway. He ain't never got a ticket, and I ain't never found no gold, but I guess if we're both incredibly persistent we'll get our way someday."

Jeff Byrd, the track's general manager, would agree with the old man and his son. "You have to be incredibly persistent," Byrd said. "We don't have a waiting list. We tried that, and it didn't work. One year we had a waiting list of 84,000 fans wanting Winston Cup tickets. You can't deal with that. We don't have a lottery, either. We tried that, and it didn't work.

"What we do," Byrd declared, "is sell you a ticket if we have one. Sometimes when a person dies and he hasn't willed his tickets, we get them back. We sell them to someone else. We don't keep tickets and we don't sell to ticket agencies. Our future is taking care of the fans, and we want race fans to have our tickets."

That's why you have to be persistent. To get a ticket to just a Winston Cup Series race at Bristol is impossible. A season ticket entitles you to NASCAR Busch Series races along with NASCAR Winston Cup Series events. In August, 65,000 campers show up for the Cup event. "We must have something for these people to do each night,"

Byrd said. "We try hard. We don't charge for parking on the speedway property. We like to do things for our fans."

Evelyn Hicks, director of ticketing operations, has worked for the speedway since January 1988. She said there has always been a demand for Bristol tickets, especially for the August race. She laughs when she says: "And the people who get tickets are usually so appreciative. Why, I got a jar of moonshine from one customer who received tickets. There was a thank-you note with it. "Big baskets of flowers and boxes of candy arriving for the girls in the ticket office are common.

"Race fans are nice people," Hicks said. "We get a lot of presents. Our biggest problem is that we don't always have something to sell. People call all day long wanting tickets, especially to the August race. We tell them their best bet is to try to get season tickets."

The ticket agents in the ticket office are busy each race week selling tickets to the NASCAR Busch Series race, the preliminary to the Winston Cup event. "We are also busy working out problems for people," Hicks noted. "We have to have death notices with wills to transfer tickets, and we must have copies of divorce papers to change the names of whom the tickets are registered with. Then some people show up and say the dog ate their tickets, or that they lost them, or they accidentally threw them away. We realize such things can happen, and we have a system to handle these situations."

There are ticket holders in 48 states and several foreign countries. The last time tickets were available, 52,000 sold in less than four hours.

Someday maybe the old man of the hills will find gold, and maybe his son will get tickets to a Bristol race. Until then, both will remain incredibly persistent. Neither of them has a choice.

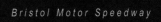

THE TENTH LEGION

(Opposite Page) Darrell Waltrip (here with country music artist T.G. Shepard), with 12 trips to victory lane, is Bristol Motor Speedway's all-time NASCAR Winston Cup Series race winner.

(Left) Junior Johnson (here talking to driver Neil Bonnett) is the speedway's undisputed winner as both a car owner and driver. While he won just once while behind the wheel, he directed his drivers to 20 additional victories.

The ancient Roman Empire conquered the entire known world and kept it subjugated for five centuries. Most historians agree that of all the Roman legions, there was none to match the Tenth. Generation after generation, in country after country, against vast armies, there was always the Tenth, and the Tenth grew and fed upon itself. An outfit such as this can exist in any facet of human existence, though it is less common in organizations other than the military.

The winner's circle at Bristol Motor Speedway is an example. Only the best – the "NASCAR Tenth Legion," you might be inclined to say – are drawn from among the army of NASCAR Winston Cup Series troops and make it through the honored barrier where race winners go. The names of those crowned include: Petty; Earnhardt; Waltrip; Pearson; Allison; Wallace; Elliott; Kulwicki; Martin, Gordon; Yarborough; Jarrett and others, in no particular order.

In the early days, the post-race marquee flashed names such as Weatherly, Paschal, Roberts, Lorenzen,

Johnson, Jarrett and others from that era. When it comes to first-place finishes, however, Darrell Waltrip, now retired from driving and pursuing a career in TV race broadcasting, is the most successful competitor at the speedway. From 1978 through 1992, he won 12 races, including seven straight in the early 1980s.

Cale Yarborough, in cars owned by Junior Johnson, won nine races at Bristol. But it's Johnson who is really the big winner at the place called "Thunder Valley." He has 21 victories to his credit, one as a driver and 20 more as a team owner. His victory total is highest of any team owner at any Winston Cup venue, topping his record of 18 at North Wilkesboro Speedway, his home track.

Johnson drove a Ford to victory at Bristol in 1965, and he's won as a team owner with Chevrolet, Oldsmobile and Buick. Eight of Waltrip's wins at Bristol were in cars owned by Johnson. Bobby Allison won two races in Johnson cars and Charlie Glotzbach won one. Yarborough won the most for Johnson, nine.

"You can't beat Bristol for sheer excitement," Johnson always said. In fact, Johnson liked the place so much that he tried to get executives at R.J. Reynolds to run The Winston special "all-star" event there. They, however, demurred, and it appears that NASCAR's All-Star race has a permanent home at Lowe's Motor Speedway near Charlotte – another Speedway Motorsports property.

That aside, Bristol Motor Speedway is just flat-out different. It's hard to fathom how much the cars are in the turns, how quickly cars get through them, then how quickly they are right back in them again. It is a very fast track, and the racing is close, which has led Yarborough to call it a "killer of a race track ... one of the most physically demanding race tracks in the world. When the race is over with, you are over with, too."

This from a guy whose middle name was "stamina" ... so tough that in a Winston Cup Series career that stretched between 1957-88 he reportedly never called upon a relief driver. Despite the challenge Bristol presents, Yarborough says he always liked running at the bullring with the steepest banks in NASCAR. "It was my kind of track. It was a hard track to run, but perfect for me. I enjoyed racing at Bristol, and when you really like a track, you usually do well on it."

"It was my kind of track. It was a hard track to run, but perfect for me. I enjoyed racing at Bristol, and when you really like a track, you usually do well on it."
— Cale Yarborough

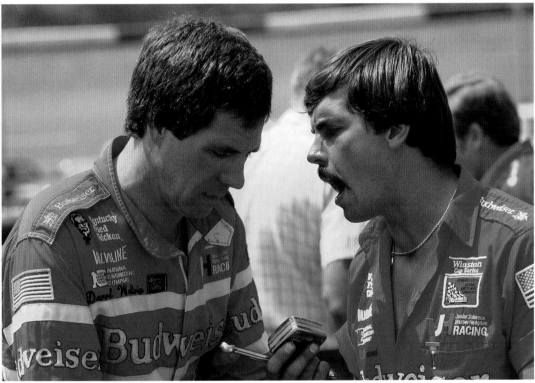

(Above) Waltrip won twice at Bristol while driving the No. 88 DiGard Racing Co. Chevrolet.

(Left) Waltrip and crew chief Jeff Hammond (right) were a winning combination at Bristol and many other places for years. In 2001, they've "teamed up" again as commentators on the Fox network's NASCAR Winston Cup Series race broadcasts.

Waltrip said he showed up at Bristol automatically liking the speedway, and he "owned" it long before Bruton Smith handed a check to Larry Carrier. It was at this track that he accomplished what he still considers to be one of his greatest feats. From the spring of 1981 through the spring of 1984 – a seven-race span – nobody but Waltrip stood in the winner's circle.

"I won seven in a row," he said. "Not seven races, but seven in a row. For three-and-a-half years I was the only one who won there."

Waltrip's apparent invincibility worked on the minds of other drivers. Supposedly, some of them began believing that no one other than Waltrip could win at Bristol. "That was part of the strategy," he told sportswriter Lori Worley of the Bristol Herald-Courier. "People believed I couldn't be beat there."

Waltrip, a native of Owensboro, Ky., lives in Franklin, Tenn., and considered Bristol his home track. "Bristol was always a very good place for me, a very special place. To be successful at that track, you always have to be driving ahead and you must have a good-handling car. We turn the track in 15 seconds. Now look at your own watch. There isn't very much you can do in 15 seconds."

The late Dale Earnhardt visited the winner's circle nine times at Bristol. Although at least two of his trips there came in the wake of controversy, even his biggest detractors have to admit Earnhardt had perfected the "art" of success at Bristol.

"You have to race the track," he said. "You can get in trouble in traffic or with lapped cars. You have got to be aware of what's going on around you. Trouble happens in a hurry, and it's usually not a one-car wreck, either."

Earnhardt, whose first of 76 Winston Cup Series victories came at Bristol in April 1979, emphasized the importance of keeping your mind on what you are doing. You can't daydream. Every second – and there are 10,800 of them in a three-hour race – counts. "We're going around that track in 15 seconds," he said. "I love going that fast, but you have to make yourself aware of everything that is going on around you. You have to depend on your crew and your spotter. You can't do it all by yourself. It is a very physical track, and once the race begins, you're at the mercy of circumstances. Driver fatigue takes its toll.

"As far as the Bristol setup, it can change, but one of the big things that the crews have to deal with is making sure they have the car high enough and stiff enough to keep it from bottoming out. If you bottom out a whole lot, then you have to worry about tearing up your bell housing or your oil pan. The racing is close. The driver can't relax for a second. If a guy gets just a little out of shape, with that many cars running that close and that fast, you can get a whole bunch of cars in trouble."

"You can get in trouble in traffic or with lapped cars. You have got to be aware of what's going on around you. Trouble happens in a hurry, and it's usually not a one-car wreck, either." — Dale Earnhardt

"Bristol is the neatest place we race. said Terry Labonte. "It is among my favorite tracks, if not my favorite. If I were given the opportunity to own a race track, I'd rather own Bristol than any of them."

"Bristol is the neatest place we race," said Terry Labonte. "It is among my favorite tracks, if not my favorite. If I were given the opportunity to own a race track, I'd rather own Bristol than any of them."

Like Earnhardt, Labonte pointed out that drivers go fast, and things can happen in a hurry. "You can get caught up in something on pit road as well as on the track. The key to winning at Bristol is to stay out of trouble, and that is difficult to do." Labonte does say he thinks the racing was better when the track was asphalt, as "then you had two grooves, one high and one low. With the concrete, it is pretty much a one-groove track, and the groove generally stays low. Bristol is a very difficult track to pass on, and the one groove makes it even more difficult."

Labonte and Earnhardt were involved in the track's biggest controversy. The incident occurred on the last lap of the 1999 summer NASCAR Winston Cup Series race. The two exchanged the lead in the event's latter stages like it was a hot potato. On the final lap, coming off turn two, Labonte drove under Earnhardt and took the lead. Earnhardt slammed into the rear of Labonte's car, turning him into the inside wall. Earnhardt drove on to victory while Labonte's car stalled against the inside wall. The crowd booed Earnhardt loudly while he went through the usual hoopla in victory lane. NASCAR officials reviewed the incident, but did not levy a fine, claiming they wanted their drivers to be able to race hard for the checkered flag in the last few laps.

> "Bristol is a quick track, and everything happens so fast. I didn't really like that, and I still don't. Sometimes, it was like you didn't really have a chance."
>
> — Richard Petty

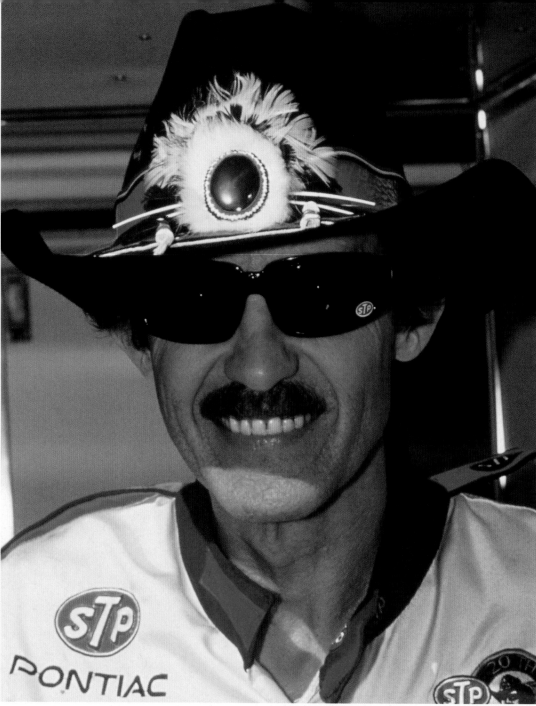

On the other hand, there is little true love of the place evidenced by Richard Petty, the NASCAR Winston Cup Series' all-time race winner, who noted, "It was not my favorite place when I was a driver, and now it is not my favorite track as a team owner." Petty won three races at the track. He started on the pole and won the Southeastern 500 in 1967, the 64th victory of his career and the 16th win of his record-breaking, 27-win season. It also helped him capture the second of his seven championships. Petty then won twice more, sweeping both races in 1975 on the way to his sixth Winston Cup title.

"Bristol is a quick track, and everything happens so fast. I didn't really like that, and I still don't. Sometimes, it was like you didn't really have a chance," Petty noted. "Don't get me wrong. It isn't that I dislike the place; it's just not one of my favorite tracks. It's an exciting track, and they are really building the place up. It's a great place for the fans. People love it because they can see everything and they like the action.

"I never won but three races at Bristol, but I usually ran well there. I remember one race when I was way out in front and my engine blew up or something. Anyway, I pulled into the pits, got out of the car and was resting on the pit road wall when the guy who was running second finally made up the laps he was behind and took the checkered flag."

"Bristol is fast and tricky, and things happen in a hurry, but I love to race there. You can't go to sleep. You have to race way ahead of your car, because things can happen and you'll be right in the middle of it all before you know it."

— Rusty Wallace

Rusty Wallace said he would just as soon race at Bristol as any place on the circuit. Could the reason be that it's where he won his first NASCAR Winston Cup Series race, the 1986 Valleydale 500, and his 50th and 51st, both in 2000? Or perhaps it's because the track reflects the driver's never-slow-down lifestyle.

"I raced on a lot of tracks around the country that are similar to Bristol when I was coming up through the ranks," he said. "Bristol is fast and tricky, and things happen in a hurry, but I love to race there. You can't go to sleep. You have to race way ahead of your car, because things can happen and you'll be right in the middle of it all before you know it. I try to drive the car ahead of myself and get my spotter to help me stay way ahead of myself."

> **"Bristol is one of the toughest places I have ever raced in my life. It takes a good, experienced driver to win on that track. It's no place for beginners."**
>
> **— Bobby Allison**

The Allison family ran Bristol as though they owned it once upon a time. Bobby (top) posted four victories, while his son, Davey (above right), and his brother, Donnie (above left), won one Winston Cup race each. Bobby's other son, Clifford, started three Bristol NASCAR Busch Series races, which meant four members of the Allison clan raced on the track. That is the most of any family in Bristol history. Also, Bobby's, Donnie's and Davey's victories made them the first three drivers from the same family to win at Bristol.

"Bristol is one of the toughest places I have ever raced in my life," Bobby Allison said. "It takes a good, experienced driver to win on that track. It's no place for beginners. Things happen in a hurry, and you have to be prepared every single lap for something to happen right in front of you – and right in front of you can mean a straightaway at Bristol."

To a degree, the Jarretts have also turned Bristol into a family affair. Ned won there when the track was young (1965), and his son, Dale (above left), is a modern-day visitor to victory circle (1997).

One of the best at Bristol is Mark Martin. "It's quite the challenge," He said. "I have a pretty good track record at Bristol. I haven't won as many races as I probably should have, but we've had our share of success at the track."

Since the driver of the Roush Racing No. 6 Ford became a permanent fixture on the Winston Cup circuit in 1988, he's won twice at Bristol. He's also finished second five times and has six pole positions – including four in a row – to his credit. The key to doing well there, he said, is having a background that includes extensive exposure to racing on the smaller tracks.

"You must have short-track experience before you come to Bristol," he said. "It is the toughest half-mile track I've ever raced on in my life. You have to be so alert and know what to do in every situation. This is where the experience comes into play. You have to know every move to make or you're going to stay in trouble all the time."

"It is the toughest half-mile track I've ever raced on in my life. You have to be so alert and know what to do in every situation. This is where the experience comes into play. You have to know every move to make or you're going to stay in trouble all the time."

— Mark Martin

"Bristol is a tough little track. You can get into more trouble there than anywhere I know, and it all happens in such a hurry. There are no coffee breaks. You must be alert every split second you are racing." — Jeff Gordon

Since his NASCAR Winston Cup Series debut in the early 1990s, Jeff Gordon seems to have won everywhere he's gone. His record includes three championships in four years (1995, 1997-98) and four wins at Bristol in 16 starts from 1993-2000. Hence, it would appear for him, the half-miler is just another race track.

"No, it is different, make no mistake about that," Gordon said. "Bristol is a tough little track. You can get into more trouble there than anywhere I know, and it all happens in such a hurry. There are no coffee breaks. You must be alert every split second you are racing."

Bill Elliott, winner of 40 NASCAR Winston Cup Series races, scored his first short-track victory in Cup competition at Bristol, taking first place in the spring race of 1988. Since then, he's won just one more race on a track of less than a mile around (Richmond, 1992).

"I would never have figured it that way," Elliott said. "I knew I could win on a short track, but winning my first short-track race at Bristol surprised me just a little. The more you run Bristol the better you like it, and the experience sure comes in handy, too."

"I knew I could win on a short track, but winning my first short-track race at Bristol surprised me just a little. The more you run Bristol the better you like it, and the experience sure comes in handy, too." — Bill Elliott

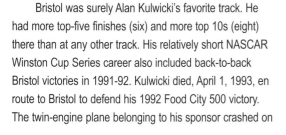

Bristol was surely Alan Kulwicki's favorite track. He had more top-five finishes (six) and more top 10s (eight) there than at any other track. It was also the only track where he won more than once as two of his five career wins came at Bristol.

Bristol was surely Alan Kulwicki's favorite track. He had more top-five finishes (six) and more top 10s (eight) there than at any other track. His relatively short NASCAR Winston Cup Series career also included back-to-back Bristol victories in 1991-92. Kulwicki died, April 1, 1993, en route to Bristol to defend his 1992 Food City 500 victory. The twin-engine plane belonging to his sponsor crashed on a hillside near the Tri-City Regional Airport in Blountville, Tenn., killing Kulwicki, two associates and the pilot.

It was a sad day in racing. Kulwicki had enjoyed some of his grandest days at the half-mile track. The Wisconsin native, who grew up racing on short tracks, had no trouble adjusting to the high banks and astonishing speeds at Bristol.

"I know my first thought was, I wondered if dead people needed shoes, because I thought I was dead. That's how hard you can hit the wall at Bristol." — David Pearson

There have been numerous spectacular accidents at the track since it opened, but probably the most horrifying occurred in a NASCAR Busch Series event on April 7, 1990. Michael Waltrip crashed into the wall and hit the gate in turn two. The accident flattened Waltrip's No. 30 Pontiac, and terrified observers could not see him anywhere in the wreckage. Then almost miraculously, Waltrip stood up and walked away from the pile of scrap that moments before was a race car.

Experienced racers said if it hadn't of been for the integrity of Waltrip's Banjo Matthews-built machine, not only would he have not escaped some physical injury, but he certainly wouldn't have been able to participate in the following day's Winston Cup event. Waltrip started 20th in the Valleydale Meats 500 and finished in the same position after running 442 laps.

Two-time NASCAR Winston Cup Series champion Joe Weatherly drove in some of the early races at Bristol before the track was banked as steeply as it is now. He also won the second

NASCAR Winston Cup Series event staged there, the Oct. 22, 1961 Southeastern 500.

When Weatherly would arrive in Bristol he would say, "I'm darn glad my car number is No. 8. That way, in the race Sunday, the fans will not be able to tell if I'm riding on my top or my wheels."

David Pearson (left), a three-time titlist, triumphed five times at Bristol and may have won on another day had he made a final practice run on Saturday afternoon. Pearson's race team worked from a spot on what is now the backstretch. He parked his street car in the infield near his race car. About the time the cars were going out for their final practice, a small fire started in the infield near Pearson's family car. He helped put the fire out and then found out that his two small sons – Ricky and Larry – had ignited the blaze!

When Pearson was driving the Cotton Owens-owned Dodge, he slammed the wall pretty hard during one of the races, and the wreck knocked him out for a few minutes. This was before the days of driving shoes, and Pearson always wore loafers. The impact of the hit was such that his loafers actually came off his feet!

When he woke up inside the car, he looked down and noticed his shoes were missing. "I know my first thought was, I wondered if dead people needed shoes, because I thought I was dead. That's how hard you can hit the wall at Bristol," he said.

Ed Clark, now president and general manager of Atlanta Motor Speedway, was the public relations director at Bristol when Lanny Hester and Gary Baker installed lights in 1978.

"The policemen were having to turn people around and send them home because we had sold every ticket. We had about 2,000 people sitting up on the banks, and probably another 2,000 or so outside the gate peering through the chain link fence so they could see half of one turn. I knew we were onto something." — Ed Clark

"I remember one of the arguments against NASCAR Winston Cup Series night racing was that you wouldn't sell any souvenir magazines because people couldn't see to read them at night," Clark recalled. "Hester and Baker weighed everything and figured they didn't have anything to lose because they were not selling that many tickets. We knew instantly it was a hit with the drivers. At the same time, there was some concern over running those speeds at night under the lights."

Clark said the thing he remembers most is that 30 minutes after the Aug. 26, 1978 Volunteer 500 started there were still people trying to get into the track. "The policemen were having to turn people around and send them home because we had sold every ticket. We had

about 2,000 people sitting up on the banks, and probably another 2,000 or so outside the gate peering through the chain link fence so they could see half of one turn. I knew we were onto something. It is hot during the days at Bristol in August, and that was one of the reasons we were not drawing fans. I remember I put a thermometer outside the press box, and when the race started it was 68 degrees and very comfortable. I guess it was the beginning of the ticket boom at Bristol."

The lights seemed to put even more emphasis on earning a trip to victory lane. And to win at Bristol surely inducts a driver into racing's Tenth Legion, a most distinguished group at a most prestigious track. ∎

(Above left) PR director Ed Clark (left) knew Gary Baker (right) made the right call when he lit the track up and made the August weekend a nighttime affair.

(Sequence) Photographer Ray Shough caught Michael Waltrip's accident during a 1990 Busch Series race. It has gone down as one of the most famous incidents at Bristol. Waltrip emerged unscathed and went on to race the next day!